Contents

Foreword

It is always a pleasure to talk with Alex Frazier or to read material prepared by him. This publication gives a very special pleasure.

In addition to his own lively and creative concepts, the author treats us to a wide array of viewpoints from such diverse sources as James Baldwin, Thoreau, Whittier, Dewey, Piaget, Christopher Jencks, Horace Mann, Audubon, Mark Twain and Yehudi Menuhin . . . to mention just a handful of the several score who are selectively quoted throughout the text.

This work represents Alexander Frazier's attempt to describe what he calls an "equal rights curriculum for all children." He uses the rubrics of "adventuring," "mastering," and "associating" as the organizing elements of the proposed curriculum.

This is, to say the least, an ambitious venture and one which the reader will find stimulating, perhaps even dismaying at times, but certainly well worth reading in any event.

Set aside time to savor and to enjoy fully the language of expression as well as the ideas which Professor Frazier sets forth in the following pages. You'll be glad you did.

DELMO DELLA-DORA, President 1975-1976
Association for Supervision
and Curriculum Development

A Need for Newness

All men and women are created equal. We seem to agree on that. But what about children? As we look around us today, we are newly conscious of children's rights and their violation. Some children plainly have better chances than others to grow up strong and whole. And such unevenness prevails in almost every realm of being.

Need this be true of schooling? That is what concerns us here.

We believe that we can and must do something about discrepancies in the quality of children's education. Thus, we are proposing a curriculum that will be good for *all* children. However, before we lay out our proposals, we will try to answer some sensible questions. Who most needs a new curriculum—and why? Who cares? What may stand in our way?

Where We Come From

The statewide system of free schools for children proposed by Thomas Jefferson in his *Plan for Education in Virginia* (1779) was designed to realize two objectives. Access to three years of reading, writing, and arithmetic would render members of the electorate "safe" to serve as the "ultimate guardians of their own liberty." And to protect the commonwealth and the republic against the dearth of talent predicted by some critics of egalitarianism, the ablest children were to be "raked from the rubbish" each year for further education.

1

By the mid-1800's the tone of support had become less condescending and more fervent. In his *Tenth Annual Report* (1846) as secretary of the Massachusetts State Board of Education, Horace Mann contended that

> . . . the natural life of an infant should be extinguished as soon as it is born, or the means should be provided to save that life from being a curse to its possessor; and, therefore, every State is morally bound to enact a code of laws legalizing and enforcing infanticide or a code of laws establishing free schools.

From the larger perspective of *Leaves of Grass* (1855), Walt Whitman called for redemption of the outcast and the underdog ("Whoever degrades another degrades me") as well as an enlargement of social responsibility:

> I speak the password primeval, I give the sign of democracy,
> By God! I will accept nothing which all cannot have their
>   counterpart of on the same terms.[1]

The scene was set. Universal education was well on its way to being accepted as a personal right and a public responsibility.

By the end of our first hundred years, in most of the states the struggle to secure free schools had been won. Our second century, if we view it as a whole, may be seen as having been taken up with realization of the free school dream. We must give ourselves credit where it is due. Today all our children are in school. Moreover, they go to school twice as many days each year as did the children of 1876. Our older youth, most of them, are in school, too. And half our high school graduates continue for a year or more of higher education.

Thus today when we talk of equal opportunity for learning, we are not thinking about money and numbers.[2] Our focus is on something else. The new challenge is surely as dramatic and perhaps as difficult of realization. But it is different in kind from public school support and total enrollment.

The new challenge before us may be phrased in several ways. Children—all children—have a right to learn what is taught. All children have a right to successful teaching. Equal access to successful teaching belongs to all children. Theirs is the right to learn whatever it

---

1 Walt Whitman. "Song of Myself." In: *Poems.* New York: Modern Library, 1921. pp. 44-45.

2 Except where "preschoolers" are concerned. As a society we have yet to decide who is going to look out for the very young.

takes to keep options open to further learning. Some of us may contend that all children have a right to learn whatever anyone can learn that will enrich or enlarge human experience.

At its simplest the new challenge could be put this way: All children have the same right to do well in school. In its most complex form, the challenge might read as follows: All children have an equal right to profit fully from a broadly based school program.

Make no mistake about it. As far as our society is concerned, this is the challenge of challenges. And whether we are ready or not, we must go forward to meet it. The reasons we have offered in the past for not having been able to teach all children equally well are proving less and less defensible. To the ears of an increasingly alert public, even our best arguments have begun to sound like alibis for inaction. One by one, our escape hatches are being closed down. (See Exhibit 1.)

Exhibit 1. When Children Can Learn: A Series of Positions

Positions	Professional Responses to the Positions
1. Children differ in how much they can learn. *The genetic theory* (1915 on)	We must vary our expectations in terms of native intelligence. Bright children deserve to be accelerated or given enriched programs, slow children need to be relieved of pressure by being judged on the basis of individual progress or by being placed in special classes.
2. Children vary in their readiness for certain kinds of learning. *Growth and development approach* (1930 on)	We need to think of children in terms of what they are able to do. Given a rich environment in school and many opportunities to interact with it, children can be trusted to select what they need to move ahead at their own pace toward development of their potential, whatever it may be.
3. Children are open to new knowledge to the extent that they feel secure and strong in themselves. *Self-concept theory* (1945 on)	We must help children maintain or develop "I-can-do-it" attitudes. Some children come to us already confident of their ability to succeed, but others have been inflicted with negative self-images that must be replaced before they can do well in school.
4. Children develop innate potential for learning as a result of social stimulation and interaction. *Social forces theory* (1960 on)	We must intervene early to enrich the experience of children from culturally impoverished environments—or work to train parents to do so. If we are unable to get results in these directions, we should try hard to compensate for deprivation damage.
5. Children come to school equipped by nature to learn what needs to be learned. *Natural powers theory* (1975)	Our job is to support learning by making possible the active exercise of natural endowment. Children will develop their powers whether or no, but schools can help by fostering the purposeful learning of needed skills and understandings.

Also new charges are being framed against us that may seem at first glance to have less to do with failure to teach than with miseducation. Perhaps we have taught some things too well. Have we wasted the time of some children by overteaching basic skills and underteaching meaningful applications and critical appreciation? To what extent have schools supported the sex role stereotyping that diminishes options both for girls and for boys? Are we really trying to teach any children some of the things that could and perhaps should be learned about the world around them and within them?

Against this background, it may be well to remind ourselves once again of the extent to which success in school is denied to some of our children. Teaching, we will agree, must be defined to encompass deciding what needs to be learned. We are talking about planning a curriculum as well as implementing it through teaching. For whom is our present curriculum unequal? Who are its victims? In short, who most needs a better curriculum and more successful teaching?

Children Who Are Taught Too Little

The children oftenest in our thoughts when we consider problems of teaching are those whom we have come to term nonlearners. No matter how hard we try, some children just do not learn very much. And we do try. New ways of organizing children for learning, new ways of staffing, new layouts of teaching space, new approaches to parents, new methods and materials—we welcome anything and everything that seems to promise help. Sometimes we have a moment of excitement. It looks like we may have gained a toehold. But when the sweat evaporates, there they still are, looking out the window, daydreaming . . . head down on the desk, resting . . . pulling or punching another child, trying to relate somehow to someone . . . or looking listlessly at the worksheet before them, waiting for the bell to ring. Despite everything we learn how to do, some of the children we try to teach are taught too little. We know these children well, and their families and their neighborhoods.

Minority Children

Children who come from subcultures of one kind or another are among those who may have a hard time in school. Non-whites and non-North European ethnics, especially when the home language is other than English (or other than school English), often seem to send us children who differ in more ways than we can count. Rich as a subculture may be in exotic foods, music, dress, customs and holidays, heroes, literature, and the like, we may find its contributions difficult to relate to our ongoing concerns.

Children from cultural minorities seem to be receiving a better deal in school now than they once did. We no longer talk of deprivation or deficiency (or anyway we try not to) and have made room for racial-ethnic content that supplements common learnings. Some children are being taught first in their mother tongue (Spanish, Navajo, French) and then in English. But still and all, minority children continue to be taught too little.

Children Who Live in the Wrong Place

Inner-city, village, and up-the-hollow children do less well in school than children from the suburbs and small cities of America. Sixth graders in a downtown school often test two or three years behind those in the rest of the district. Sixth graders in suburban schools will be two or three years ahead of national norms. Rural children may go to school every day the buses run. But, if test results are any clue to teaching competence, we may wonder what they find when they get there.

Whatever it is that is at work, some children grow up in neighborhoods or communities that seem to predispose them to success in school while others do not. Obviously we have little or no control over the factors that may be involved. All we can be sure of is that the child who grows up in the wrong place will be taught less in schools as they are now than will the child who lives in another place.

Poor Children

Children from welfare families or families whose breadwinner holds a low-paying job quite often do not do too well in school. Apparently school strikes some poor families, parents and children alike, as unrelated to either needs or interests. As we view it, poverty sometimes seems to create a culture of its own in which things as they are may carry more weight than things as they might be.

No doubt the promise of schooling as a way out of the slums or off the worn-out farms of backwoods America remains real and rewarding for many poor children. But for others, going to school is a bore and a burden. Such children learn little of what we try to teach.

Working-class Children

Children born into working-class families tend to do less well in school than children from middle-class homes. It is not a matter of money. When they have employment, truck drivers, spindle machine operators, and carpenters earn plenty. But the values and models before their children seem to favor success in arenas beyond the school, such as holding their own with others, excelling in a variety of highly active recreational pursuits, making their own money, gaining a good start toward an early marriage, and, in general, getting out on their own as soon as possible.

Some of these children do well enough in school. But many more do not care whether they do well or not. Many of them could do much better; their IQ's are proof of that. We are distressed when, try as we will, we succeed in teaching working-class children as little as we do.

Dumb Kids

Some children are not too able to begin with and thus will not learn much in school. As we all know, the proportion of what the public might call dumb kids can be expected to vary from one school community to the next. The type and degree of disablement among children with lowered capacity to learn (this is the kind of language we prefer) also varies.

Programs and provisions for less-able learners are always under review. At present we are returning some children formerly sequestered in classes of their own to regular classes for part or even all of the day. And we are taking a closer look at whose children are most likely to be taught apart. While we do not now know what more we could do about it, we acknowledge that so-called dumb kids are taught little in our schools—perhaps too little.

Boys

Boys often have a hard time in school as it now is. Any way we slice it, the children who do not measure up are mostly male. Boys have more trouble learning to read. Long after most girls are solving arithmetic problems in their heads, a good many boys are still counting on their fingers. Boys can't seem to stay within the lines. They tend to dawdle over their work. The child waiting to see the principal is almost certain to be a boy.

We are aware of several good reasons why this should be so. Growth-wise, nature has given girls the jump on boys. Most teachers of children are women and this may make a difference. Out-of-school socialization for boys from some segments of society can conflict with the behavior demanded in school. Whatever the cause, we know that many boys are taught too little.

As we think about trying to do better by all these children, we may become mildly depressed. Minority children, children who live in the wrong place, poor children, the children of working-class families, dumb kids, boys—how many children there are for whom successful teaching is not equally available. And, as indicated in the thumbnails of these children, conditions and causes over which we have little or no control seem mostly to blame.

Yet we are committed, all of us, both personally and professionally, to try for a breakthrough. And we have made gains. Two generations of attention to the psychology and sociology of school success have given us a position today that promises to be more liberating than its predecessors (Exhibit 1), each of which in its turn has been more open to the impact of education. If we read disability out of our vocabulary and refocus instead on the natural powers of the child, perhaps we will be able to do something more about the better teaching of the undertaught. A better curriculum may already be on the way.

Those Who May Be Overtaught

Children who learn too little of what is taught will remain our first concern. But equal rights must be defined to apply to everybody. Thus, we ask ourselves whether we have in school other children whose needs are being met inadequately by the present program. Or to return to our controlling question, are there still more victims of an inequitable curriculum and unsuccessful teaching?

We propose to contend first that there may be quite a large number of children who suffer from being overtaught. In later sections we will identify a couple of other groups who may also be considered victims of an outmoded curriculum and poorly intentioned teaching.

Children Who Already Know It

When we receive a group of children, we may find that some already know part of what we are prepared to teach. For example, a few first graders may have learned how to read. At later levels more than a few children may have developed skills and understandings ahead of the game. For them earlier teaching has really taken. Or having learned to be self-starters, they have ventured out on their own.

Is our program open enough to make room for these children? Suppose we are teaching in a suburban or small-city school where the median achievement in almost everything is far beyond grade norm. Do we still take all the children through study materials aimed at grade-level learning? If we do, we can be sure we are subjecting many of them to a treadmill overlearning of familiar content. Wasteful of time as well as painfully tedious, such a practice may force ahead-of-the-game children to do their serious learning outside of school.

Ready Learners

Almost every group has some children who are eager to get done whatever they are expected to do. If it is a worksheet, they will have it completed before the teacher has cleared up a last point or two for those who need to ask questions. If it is a learning packet, more than half the time these eager beavers will be able to figure out from their errors on the pretest what they need to know to be ready for the post-test. The elaborate array of activity options in between is not for them. When they need help, a little is more than enough.

But once assignments are finished, what then? Ready learners are often eager because they want to clear the decks for other undertakings—a science project perhaps or a new book or a piece of weaving already on the loom. These days more often than not such children may find themselves saddled with supplemental worksheets (enrichment) or the next learning packet (rapid transit). In either case, overlearning may preempt time that might have gone to a worthier enterprise.

Full-up Learners

Children, we may grant, can take just so much learning of any particular kind. When what we try to give them is more than they can handle, their cup runneth over. They will have had it, so to speak.

Do we sometimes waste valuable time teaching the as yet unteachable? When something is hard to learn, we may feel ourselves obliged to try to teach it. We must be cautious, of course, about lowering our expectations for learning, especially among young children. But we will concede that a great deal of time can be wasted by teaching beyond the readiness of children. This kind of overteaching is especially tempting as we try to challenge children who have proved themselves easy to teach.

When teaching does not pay off in new learning for easy learners, then we must wonder what is wrong. We have identified several kinds of children who in our terms may be overtaught. In almost every school a few children—and in some schools many children—are ahead of where they might be expected to be if we were to think in terms of grade level or achievement norms. In many schools, some children are so eager to learn that they get through before the rest begin. Many children learn easily enough but may fill up before the teacher runs down. In all these cases, teaching can be a waste of effort.

Do children for whom teaching is unsuccessful because of redundancy or prematurity have a right to something better? We may decide that a fair deal for all will have to include provision of a more truly challenging curriculum for overtaught children.

Children Who Are Mistaught

Teaching does not have to be unsuccessful to prove damaging to some children. The better the teaching of certain things, the worse for the learner. When children come to view themselves as girls or boys in ways that close down options or openings for further learning, they have been miseducated. When children discover in school that what their families do or what their subcultures have to offer is of little worth, they may be said to have been miseducated.

Are we to take on, then, the social forces that work to maintain sex role stereotypes or overplay the middle class culture at the expense of pluralism? We may be reluctant to lock horns with what could look to us like society itself. But if we can remember that half of us are women and most of us work for a living and one out of every three or four of us as Americans belongs to some sort of identifiable racial-ethnic minority, then the task may not seem so great. Our first task is to raise our own consciousness of what continued miseducation can mean to children.

Many Girls—and Some Boys

Debate over the equal rights amendment to the Constitution has sensitized us to inequities in the legal status of women. The affirmative action movement is alerting us to inequities on the employment scene. In the schools we are examining library books, textbooks, and even dictionaries for sex bias. Even now, as new books for children appear, heroines are more adventurous than of old and boys are allowed to shed a tear or two. No doubt in time mathematics textbooks will include problems that call for measuring the bedroom for carpeting, using a calory chart, and adapting recipes. Authors with a social studies series under revision are surely seeking companions for Betsy Ross and Clara Barton. These are all changes that need to be made.

But we have a long way to go before we can really get a good hold on the problem of sex role stereotyping in school. A broader range of models can be provided by study materials and should be—and by TV programs and, indeed, by life itself. Yet meanwhile the school may seem to be in unconscious partnership with patterns of behavior that can prove limiting to many girls and some boys.

Preference for certain subject fields as against others can surface early and become progressively more binding. Girls fear mathematics and find science boring: boys disdain the arts and have a hard time relating books to their most absorbing interests. In the past, boys may have escaped into the excitement of sports and games. We should not be too surprised to find that this is almost the only field of school achievement which is under direct challenge on the basis of equal rights.

Perhaps all the subject fields do need to be reexamined. However, at present some of the attempts to think about sex bias from this vantage point seem tangential. Since teachers of children are mostly women who were in their time turned off by science and mathematics, what we may need is more men teaching children. Or if more sports stories were included in the readers, boys might like to read better. Ideas like these may strike us as unlikely to make much difference.

What is called for, if we are to attack sex bias head on, is something that goes far beyond providing better role models in school and equalizing preferences among the subject fields. We must look at the impact of the curriculum as a whole. The truth is that many if not most programs for children have been so thoroughly devitalized that only passive responses are called for or valued. Success within this curriculum reinforces the worst or least of the behaviors once identified and now rejected as feminine: offering the right answer, following the proper form, staying within the lines, getting everything done, and handing it in on time.

Much of what children have to learn is taken for granted. The pressure is always toward conventionalization of content and procedures. A century and a half ago Goethe was lamenting that the children of Weimar were "prematurely tamed," with all that was natural and wild and original ruled out of their behavior. If we want a curriculum full of excitement and challenge for our children, both girls and boys, we are going to have to work very hard at reconstruction of what we now have at hand.

Children of Little Account

Can children learn in school that they and their families do not amount to much? If so, then we would have to agree that they have been mistaught.

None of us would want to contend for a curriculum that is demonstrably class-biased. But we may be slow to recognize class bias when we see it. We have had help in coming to grips with racial-ethnic oversights. We are now being alerted to some aspects of sex bias in school. Who is helping us work through the dimensions of middle-class control of our curriculum? The best help we have had comes from a study that at first glance may have looked to some of us like an attack on the value of schooling but which turns out to be something else again. Quit thinking about education as a get-ahead-in-the-world kind of enterprise, Jencks is advising. The school should leave income equalization to legislative action, and turn instead to developing a curriculum that celebrates and fosters human fulfillment.[3]

Emphasis on getting ahead is only one aspect of class bias. For the most part, the contributions of the working class, its heroes as well as its achievements, are never front and center in our schools except when it is tall tale time (Paul Bunyan, John Henry, and the like). Jack

[3] Christopher Jencks. *Inequality: A Reassessment of the Effect of Family and Schooling in America.* New York: Basic Books, 1972.

London, if he comes into view at all, is disposed of as a writer of animal stories. The labor movement might as well never have happened.

More to the point perhaps is that after some attention to community helpers, work as work receives, or has received, little room in schools for children. "Even in grade one I think we all knew we were going to cut wood and fish and trap and hunt all our lives," recalls one Indian leader, "and we'd already learned a whole lot about these things by doing them."[4] For him and his friends, school was a world apart. What the Indian children had already learned was not valued; what they now mainly learned in school was that they were dumb.

Career education may be making a difference. The peril there, of course, is that once again by comparison the world that many children inhabit will be revealed as of little account.

Children Who Are Not Taught Some Things at All

At this point, we may feel that we have gone about as far as we can or should go in searching out inequities of curriculum and instruction. Yet there is one more aspect of equal rights to which we really must address ourselves.

We can hardly dispute the fact that some children have a much richer and more relevant school experience than others. Here it is not a question of being undertaught, overtaught, or mistaught. Many children are just not taught some things at all.

And perhaps we could even claim that most children in our schools today are not taught some things that they need to be taught.

Rather than argue these charges and claims, let us be content here to list some of the kinds of learning that we feel may be unavailable at present to many or most children and to which they might be thought to have a right. As we develop our proposals in succeeding chapters, we will return to this list:

The environment: What sustains an ecosystem, what alters it . . . population and pollution . . . designing an environment good for all living things . . . wilderness and its enjoyment . . . austerity and survival

---

4 Wilfred Pelletier and Ted Poole. *No Foreign Land: The Biography of a North American Indian.* New York: Pantheon Books, a division of Random House, Inc., 1973. Copyright © 1973.

Full range of the arts: More than singing folksongs, coloring with crayons . . . architecture, city planning, landscaping . . . sculpture . . . furniture and clothing . . . dance and drama . . . the literature and music of the Orient, of Africa

Love and friendship: Living with others and liking it . . . sensitivity to others . . . talking about how we feel . . . skills of working together . . . making and keeping friends . . . welcoming newcomers

Media and the marketplace: How advertising works . . . what children buy . . . why TV offers the programs it does . . . role of public television . . . newspapers . . . radio . . . consumer protection

Play and playfulness: Learning to make the most of physical activity . . . movement and body management . . . walking, running, swimming . . . tumbling . . . other sports and games . . . festivals . . . recreation in general

Political action: When change is needed . . . how people get together . . . the role of disagreement and debate . . . information and communication . . . lawmakers, the law, the courts

Self-understanding: How children grow up . . . something about socialization . . . children and grownups . . . individual differences . . . interests and talents . . . my groups . . . who am I and what do I want to be?

Value clarification: Testing guidelines to action . . . competing goods . . . today and tomorrow . . . yours, mine, and ours . . . justice, generosity . . . what is really important

The world of work: How goods and services are created . . . varieties of work . . . interdependence . . . child labor . . . advances in welfare of workers . . . a rising standard of living . . . when hard times come

A world view: Why we seek peace . . . getting together on common problems . . . developing nations . . . nationhood, the United Nations . . . richness of world cultures . . . in prospect: some elements shared by many nations.

Some of us may charge this list with a lack of novelty. We have talked about many of these areas and items a lot, that is true, and may have touched on some of them with children as well as we could. We may be forced to reduce our contention that these are areas where most children are not taught at all. Can we settle for claiming that the areas and items on this list that are touched on are often only half taught?

What we are trying to establish hardly needs further debate. We will surely agree that we may be expected to include more attention to a number of largely neglected areas of learning as we work to develop a curriculum that will be equally good for all children.

For whom is our present curriculum unequal? As we have tried to answer this question, we have identified four sets of victims (see Exhibit 2). First, some children are undertaught. They do not learn what we intend to teach. Second, some children are overtaught. Their time is wasted through the redundancy or prematurity of our teaching. Third, some children are mistaught. They learn what we did not mean to teach. Finally, many children are not taught at all, or are only half taught, some of the things that matter most. Access to the fullness of our human heritage is never really theirs.

Exhibit 2. What Happens to Children Who Are Victims of Unequal Teaching?

Type of Inequality	Results of Inequality
Children who are undertaught	Fail to learn what they could learn
	Fall behind others and become discouraged
	Develop dislike for school
	May escape from schooling at earliest opportunity
	Find themselves boxed in by lack of education
Children who are overtaught	Waste time in overlearning
	Become bored with school
	May develop distaste for learning
	May fail to find themselves
	Find themselves boxed in by lack of education
Children who are mistaught	Limit interest to subjects thought appropriate to sex role or social status
	May learn to dislike or fear some subjects
	Fail to develop broad base for further learning
	Grow up half educated
	Find themselves boxed in by lack of education
Children who are not taught some things at all	Respond less fully to total environment
	May develop prejudices against the arts
	Function at less than best in some aspects of human relationships
	May remain ignorant of important realms of human experience
	Find themselves boxed in by lack of education

Forces in Support of Inequality

In trying to raise the level of our own consciousness, we may do well to reconsider a number of historical forces sometimes charged with supporting a constricted curriculum for children and poor teaching. Our own viewpoint is that none of these operates today as perhaps it once did. At the same time, we must grant that history has a way of holding on to us in patterns of behavior of which we may scarcely be aware. All too often we do not know where we have come from. Thus, we cannot consciously free ourselves of old ways of thinking that could prove disabling today.

School as Middle-class Agency

Jefferson saw the public school as an agency for finding talent to serve the state. In the same way, the school could recruit for the business and industrial establishment. Schools for the common folk may always have served this purpose. A decision whether a child should continue schooling or go to work often marked the end of childhood. Today, in some countries, the decision is over which children are to go to one kind of school, which to another.

In any case, the criterion for selection was success in previous schooling. Those who made it were privileged to join their betters. "The spread of education," as Mann remarked in his *Twelfth Annual Report* (1848), "by enlarging the cultivated class or caste, will open a wider area over which the social feelings will expand; and, if this education should be universal and complete, it would do more than all things to obliterate factitious distinctions in society."

Is the screening function still at work in our schools? If so, the survival of selective teaching within a narrow curriculum can be better understood. But how sad a situation that would be. School success is not as sure a way to a distinguished career as we may once have thought, Jencks contends. And all of us agree that personal fulfillment should loom larger than getting ahead in the world as the controlling purpose of childhood education.

Methods-oriented Teacher Preparation

In the past at least, the education of teachers of children may have been oriented toward how to teach at the expense of learning more about the nature of children, subject matter and its possibilities, and the needs of society. Curriculum making, which depends on these latter under-standings, was seen as a large-scale and official undertaking that lay outside the province as well as the competence of the elementary school teacher. The message to come through must have been much like that received by the British cavalrymen at Balaklava: "Theirs not to reason why,/Theirs but to do and die."

Historians tell us that the charge of the Light Brigade was heroic but useless. Could the same be said about much of the hard work of generations of teachers? Surviving the county examinations over the common branches and the normal school courses in the teaching of handwriting, spelling, and arithmetic, teachers of bygone times must have been disappointed to discover that not all children were like them. A good many children would not or could not learn the little that was taught; more than a few must have been bored to death by the relentless overteaching of the fundamentals. To what extent teachers were uneasy about the possibility of misteaching some children or regretful at not knowing enough to expand the constricted curriculum to include more of the human heritage, we cannot say.

Commercialized Study Materials

"The following books and none others, shall be used in the several schools, viz.: Alden's *Spelling Book,* first & second part, *New Testament, American Preceptor,* Murray's *Sequel to the English Reader,* Murray's *Abridgement of English Grammar,* and Dabol's *Arithmetick.*" So read the regulations in force in 1800 for the instruction and government of the Providence, Rhode Island, public schools.[5]

Would we seem ungrateful if we wondered about the impact of textbooks on the constriction of the curriculum for children? In sober fact, more often than not textbooks *were* the curriculum in the past. Even today the world over, half or more of all books published each year are produced for school use. In this country, more teachers than we would expect may begin whatever they plan to do by asking children to open their books. The resources of the school library (or instructional materials center) may be rich and varied, but first things must come first. Is the first thing still the textbook in too many classrooms?

[5] Report of the Committee for Revising the School Regulations. *Centennial School Report, 1899.* In: E. P. Cubberley, editor. *Readings in History of Education.* Boston: Houghton Mifflin Company, 1920. p. 548. Copyright © Board of Trustees, Leland Stanford Junior University. Reprinted by permission.

Conventionalization of Content

An early nineteenth century teacher's manual for Worcester's *Primer* provides us with this example of what the specification of content looks like when combined with methodology ("Nature's method" of presenting words first, letters later):

Teacher (turning to page 15 and pointing to picture). What is this?

Child. A man.

T. That is the picture of a man. Would you not like to know the word man?

C. Yes.

T. (pointing to the word). There it is. Look at it well that you may know it again. Now do you think you shall know it?

To this question the child generally answers yes.

T. (turning to page 17). Which of these words (pointing to man, dog, cat) is man?

Unless the child has been brought up in habits of attention by his parents, his heedlessness will be apparent by his ignorance of the word. And this will generally be the case. So, turning back to page 15, the teacher can say,

T. You are wrong. See, it does not look like that. You should give more attention. Look at it again (page 15; trace the form of the word with a pointer). Are you sure you will know it now?

C. Yes.

Most children will now know the word. But a few will be found so heedless as still not to have given any attention. With these there will be some difficulty.[6]

Here teacher training and textbook publication may seem about to unite to reduce curriculum to its ultimate unit, the word. Less than a century later, the word list would be elevated into the arbiter of arbiters for determining the concept level of what was published for children in both library books and textbooks.

Is there any point really in trying to fix blame for curriculum constriction on any force in particular? The whole drift of deciding what to teach children has always been toward conventionalization and devitalization. From time immemorial, the content of children's learning has been agreed upon. It is the first steps in everything, more or less. Spelling these out leads to a kind of curriculum that calls for passive

---

[6] Quoted by George B. Emerson. *The Schoolmaster.* Boston: Fowle and Capen, 1843. pp. 420-21.

learning. We noted this phenomenon when we were discussing the question of misteaching. Nobody or nothing is to blame. In the midst of life, there is the school for children. And unless we watch it most vigilantly, this school can become a paper-and-pencil prison.

New Respect for Children as Learners

Too many children are victims today of unequal teaching within a residual or rock-bottom curriculum. The forces that maintain the inequities of curriculum constriction and selective teaching have a long history, and some of them are no doubt still operative. Our first challenge is to look the facts straight in the face. Before we can do much about it, we have to understand what is going on. With heightened awareness of the problem, we may be expected to look about us for help in developing an equal rights curriculum that will provide us a better base for successful teaching.

One source of help is the concept of natural powers. After years of trying to identify what makes for success in learning and modifying our ideas to move closer to a vital role for the school (see Exhibit 1 once again), we may be ready to grant that what we do in school bears directly on what children can do. The liberating force of this idea has yet to be fully understood or written into practice. But it could clear away, perhaps once and for all, our dependence on factors over which we have no control for explanations of why children can or cannot learn.

The Gifts of Nature

We are all born with what it takes to function as human beings. From the word go, we begin to use nature's gifts to make sense out of our world, gain satisfaction from it, and choose rewardingly among its many goods. We are able to reach out for, take in, and make something of whatever is around us. We are able to establish bonds with others and engage in common undertakings. We can create plans and see them through; we can predict and puzzle over outcomes. In short, we are born human, with the natural powers that enable us to make the most of life.

Some of us will grow up where there may be more to draw upon in the exercise of our powers. Thus, what we do may become more effective and fulfilling. Schooling, to the extent that it provides an environment arranged to nourish and strengthen our powers, must certainly make a difference. Yet throughout human history most of us have grown up with no more to work with than the items and events of everyday existence. And the exercise of our powers has enabled us to realize a respectable range of human purposes. Interaction with the world, whatever it may contain, will give us what we have to have to create an environment that sustains us. So goes our thinking about the function of natural powers.

Biology of Learning Behavior

We can count on children to develop competence if we give them a chance. Our faith that this is so has been the most tenacious tenet of our creed, lost sight of often enough, it is true, but enduring nonetheless wherever teachers have been in daily contact with learning children. "I see him bright, eager, vigorous, carefree, completely absorbed in the present, rejoicing in abounding vitality," Rousseau remarks as he urges on us a vision of the complete child. "I see him in the years ahead using senses, mind, and power as they develop from day to day. I view him as a child and he pleases me. I think of him as a man and he pleases me still more."[7]

Today our faith in natural powers is newly underwritten by the findings of behavior biologists like Konrad Lorenz and Nicholass Tinbergen, recent winners of the Nobel prize. Autonomous drives originate as a function of the organic system. Animal and human behavior has dependable roots in the central nervous system. In short, the disposition to learn comes with the creature. Investigation of what innate structure prepares children to learn has opened up a whole new view of language acquisition. We discover that children come to us already highly competent in applying the rules of the sentence-making game.[8]

Intelligence: the Outcome of Interaction

Even more to the point is our rediscovery of Piaget's central message. Children move in invariant order from one stage of intellectual functioning to the next, enabled to do so by the fulfillment of internal structures. Interaction with the environment is as necessary for intellectual maturation as it is for physical growth. Mind is a product of such interaction. Intelligence develops as children act on what is around them and make it truly their own. "The essential functions of intelligence

[7] William Boyd, translator and editor. *The Emile of Jean Jacques Rousseau: Selections.* New York: Teachers College Press, 1962. pp. 65-66.

[8] Well summarized in: Courtney B. Cazden. *Child Language and Education.* New York: Holt Rinehart and Winston, Inc., 1972.

consist in understanding and in inventing, in other words, in building up structures by structuring reality."[9]

What this all adds up to is a new or renewed respect for the child as a learner. We can count on children to learn—if we give them a chance. Children must be free to use their powers if the powers are to develop. Children must be mostly active rather than passive in learning. And if the school does not allow their powers to be exercised, then children will have to depend upon out-of-school environment for sustenance. Reliance on nonschool experience for the stuff of learning obviously reduces effectiveness and fulfillment in the growth of natural powers.

Will we be able to accept the challenge of reordering the school environment to optimize the exercise of natural powers? Do we know how to make an environment that combines open exploration with the assurance that children will find there what is most nourishing? Are we willing to accept responsibility for designing an equal rights curriculum that will make it possible for all children to learn what we intend to teach?

New Insights into How To Teach

If we can summon up energy to think beyond present practice, we should find the concept of natural powers helpful in charting the dimensions of a more equitable program for children. Another source of help is the new supply of insights into how to teach. Over the past 15 to 20 years, we have accumulated a good deal of evidence that when we put our minds to it, we can do better than we have done in the past. For our purposes here it may be unnecessary to do more than offer a few notes to remind us of where we have been working most diligently in recent years.

Maximization of Role of Interest

Probably the most enduring contribution of the science and mathematics modernization projects of the early and mid-60's came from the emphasis they gave to learning through inquiry and discovery. The ends spelled out in the renovation of content were to be held in mind by

---

[9] Jean Piaget. *Science of Education and the Psychology of the Child.* Derek Coltman, translator. New York: The Viking Press, 1970. p. 27. Copyright © 1970 by Grossman Publishers, a division of Viking Penguin, Inc. Reprinted by permission.

the reeducated teacher. But children, it was decided, would gain more and hold onto it better if they arrived at what they needed to know on their own. Granted the time it takes to define concepts and frame generalizations and test them out, children would learn how to learn, too, as well as learn what they were supposed to learn about science or mathematics.

The reaffirmation of our long-held belief in the primacy for children of active learning may have come as a surprise to many persons. By this time, however, we have grown used to the fact that all of us in childhood education, oldtimers and innovators alike, support an interest base for teaching. Also, we know how to make it come off better than before. And we have new evidence that this approach really works.

Definition of Teaching Outcomes

One of the most productive fields of methodological study has been finding out how to specify teaching outcomes more precisely. In some kinds of learning, we do want children to achieve mastery. All too often in the past, we may have had only the vaguest notion of what it was, on a day-to-day basis, we were actually trying to teach. By insisting on definition of outcomes in terms of observable behaviors or testable competencies, we seem to have made a breakthrough of great significance.

No doubt we still have far to go. Sometimes we may have settled too soon for getting back from children the bits and pieces of passive learning. But in our best efforts we are turning to analysis of basic skills and concepts for more knowledge of what has to go into learning as well as into teaching. A brilliant example of the promise of this kind of analysis is found in Whimbey's reduction of "intelligence" to a set of skills that it is believed can be taught.[10]

The Promise of Environment

Another dramatic breakthrough has come in the application of reinforcement therapy to maladaptive or nonadaptive behavior. Children with disabling or disruptive ways of behaving have been rescued and returned to normal functioning with a dispatch and degree of success far beyond anything we have known before.

At present, we are not in agreement about whether the proven clinical values of this approach can be translated into the arrangement

[10] Arthur Whimbey with Linda S. Whimbey. *Intelligence Can Be Taught.* New York: E. P. Dutton & Co., Inc., 1975.

of a classroom environment that will encourage and sustain the kind of behavior we most desire. Some of the reward systems now being promulgated—pats on the head or jelly beans or time-out tokens for each act of approved behavior—obviously miss the boat. They are designed to promote low-level passive learning. We believe learning through the active exercise of natural powers to be innately rewarding. But no doubt some circumstances or contingencies do more than others to ensure the operation of natural reinforcement. The promise of environment is still there.

New insights into teaching of the kinds we have reviewed are sometimes hard to reconcile, one with another. Yet we know we will need all the strength we can muster if we are to move onto a higher level of success in teaching. Perhaps the sanest way to view these new findings is through their relationship to teaching as a whole. We may then be able to view them simply as different dimensions of successful teaching, all of them promising and all of them a part of the picture (see Exhibit 3).

Can we keep the promise of new teaching insights before us despite our doubts about some present applications? Will we be inventive in making use of new knowledge within our own framework of values and concerns? Are we resolved to stay with our testing out of new ways of teaching until we have gained all they may have to offer?

Summary and Conclusion

"As the emphasis shifts to the environment," Skinner concedes, "the individual seems to be exposed to a new kind of danger. Who is to construct the controlling environment and to what end?"[11] The answer to this fear, as the thoroughgoing environmentalist gives it, is that at least in thinking about a planned environment the option is open. Who can be held responsible for an accidental or inherited environment? What ends may it unknowingly serve? We have examined at some length the historical forces that may tend to sustain the constricted curriculum of the past. We have speculated on the ends served, unwittingly enough, by selective teaching.

If we are to design an equal rights curriculum, we must certainly acknowledge the new ends that are behind our effort. Some of these

11 B. F. Skinner. *Beyond Freedom and Dignity.* New York: Alfred A. Knopf, Inc., 1971. p. 19. Copyright © 1971 by Alfred A. Knopf, Inc.

Exhibit 3. Major Dimensions of Successful Teaching

Factors in Teaching	Elements of Teaching		
	Stimulating Interest	Setting Expectations	Shaping Behavior
Nature of children	Interested in almost everything around them, children respond well to the stimulation of new concerns.	Children need limits or boundaries and respond to the setting of these as an adult responsibility.	At the less than conscious level, environment, both physical and social, patterns behavior in many ways.
Theories of learning	Interest is the first line of approach with all learners but especially with children.	Mastery of common learnings by all children can be assured by careful planning and target teaching.	The environment can be so arranged that some kinds of behavior can be promoted, some prevented, some replaced.
Function of content	Content may be provided to satisfy interests children already have and can also be used to arouse new interests.	Some content serves to ensure common learnings thought to be needed by all children.	Experiences can be selected in part because they serve to shape or reshape behavior.
Demands of society	The dynamic quality of our society depends in part upon the diversity of our talents and interests.	Children are entitled to successful teaching of the common learnings needed by all.	Children should be taught to behave in ways that will prove personally rewarding and also will benefit society.
Role of the teacher	Present interests are built on and extended and new interests excited as a basis for much successful teaching.	Defining common learnings clearly, presenting relevant content effectively, and making sure of mastery are all part of successful teaching.	Children must be taught to behave so that their natural powers will have full expression, both for their own welfare and for ours.

have been put before us by a society or segments of it in the demand for more successful teaching of many children—the undertaught, the overtaught, the mistaught. We have stretched our awareness of new possibilities to identify content areas which are not taught at all—or only half taught—to most children today. Each of these carries within it the promise of helping realize new ends. As we have talked about new respect for the natural powers of the learner, we have noted how schooling can contribute to their development. The exercise of natural powers in an enriched environment must lead to greater effectiveness and fulfillment. These ends may surely stand as newly defined in this context.

All of us, out of our own personal and professional experience in recent years, have derived a new sense of the concerns that ought to govern our interaction with children. We hope that children will find joy in being alive in school as well as out. We hope that openness and honesty will prevail in their relations one with another and with the wider world around them. We hope that a sense of first things first will combine with reverence for life to elevate their outlook on the use and abuse of human and natural resources. We hope that responsibility for others and the need for autonomy will come into some sort of mutually supportive balance in their lives.[12]

Can we sharpen and keep before us the full range of new ends that we intend to reach in the design of an equal rights curriculum for children?

So much for the current scene. We have tried to place our endeavor in perspective. We have identified the need as we see it. We have defined some of the new knowledge that ought to help. Now to turn to the task at hand.

[12] See: Alexander Frazier. "The Quality of Life and Society in the United States." A statement prepared for ASCD, in: Robert R. Leeper, editor. *A Man for Tomorrow's World*. Washington, D. C.: Association for Supervision and Curriculum Development, 1970. pp. 62-84.

Adventuring

Adventuring—what better place to start in thinking about a better curriculum for children! Let's build anew on what we know for sure. More than anything else, children who have been unoccupied or restless or bored to death in school may need to be turned loose on the world in ways that make sense to them. Can we see what this might mean for children who have been undertaught, overtaught, mistaught, and not taught some things at all?

What Comes Naturally

In the first days of life, satisfaction of need comes from an instinctive assault upon environment. The space immediately around the infant yields to outcry, clutching, sucking—and becomes a dependably warm breast, a dry nappy, a smiling and soon-to-be familiar face. Beyond lies all the rest.

So begins the lifelong adventure of finding what we need in the world about us. "Life itself is a steady state of enormous improbability," the father of the new physiology of behavior reminds us, and what must strike us most "is the fact that organisms and species miraculously manage to stay alive."[1] Even with the "amazing facts of adaptedness" taken for granted, the process of learning to survive remains a miracle.

[1] Konrad Lorenz. *Evolution and Modification of Behavior.* Chicago: University of Chicago Press, 1965. pp. 32-33.

27

The first business of the child is to satisfy basic needs. But before long and bit by bit, the space beyond begins to offer new kinds of satisfaction. Light and shadow enliven the ceiling, and their interplay becomes absorbing. A toy dropped from the crib returns to hand. New smilers draw near and learn to play peekaboo and pick-me-up. Soon thereafter the crawler and the toddler venture abroad, seeking to make more sense out of their environment. Only then are they able to identify alternatives. The more sense, the greater the range of possible satisfactions—that is what these young explorers discover. The primary blueprint of instinctive learning gives way to purposeful learning. The aims of adventuring become many and varied. (See Exhibit 4 for some indication of dimensions.)

Our challenge is to keep adventuring in the picture for children once they have come to school. How can the exploratory urge and impulse best be sustained? What counts for most in the exercise and strengthening of natural powers? Which selected environments most deserve to be explored?

As we prepare to answer these questions as a basis for developing an equal rights curriculum, we will do well to hold fast to our awareness of what comes naturally to children. When we lose this awareness, then it is that we seem to go astray. For a long time, the primacy of interest in the education of children has been called to our attention:

Comenius (1645): "Human nature is free and hates coercion."

Locke (1693): "Curiosity in children is but an appetite after knowledge and therefore ought to be encouraged."

Rousseau (1762): "Present interest: that is the great motive impulse, the only one that leads sure and far."

Exhibit 4. A Vocabulary of Adventuring: Aims and Dimensions

attempting	exploring	pursuing	striking out
braving	groping for	questing	surveying
breaking out	inquiring	rambling	testing
daring	investigating	ranging	traveling
departing from	jaunting	roaming	trying out
discovering	journeying	roving	undertaking
encountering	launching out	searching	venturing
examining	looking around	seeking	wandering
experiencing	moving out	sightseeing	wayfaring
experimenting	prowling	spying out	

But let us review our understandings here in a fashion that may point new pathways for us.

Making the Most of Things

The poet Wordsworth recalls the "bright blue river" that ran through the fields near his childhood home:

> Oh, many a time have I, a five years' child . . .
> Made one long bathing of a summer's day;
> Basked in the sun, and plunged and basked again
> Alternate, all a summer's day, or scoured
> The sandy fields, leaping through flowery groves
> Of yellow ragwort; or . . . stood alone
> Beneath the sky, as if I had been born
> On Indian plains, and from my mother's hut
> Had run abroad in wantonness, to sport,
> A naked savage, in the thunder shower.[2]

A free run of the place helps the child make the most of a familiar environment. In the memory of adults, summertime is often recalled as free-run time—"boyhood's time of June," in Whittier's words, "When all things I heard or saw,/ Me, their master, waited for"—the squirrel, the mole, the pickerel pond, the walnut slopes. A summer storm in Cornwall transforms the beach for "Ralph, Vasey, Alastair, Biddy, John, and me" into a new "water-world/ Of rain and blizzard, sea and spray"—and in recollection the poet Betjeman prays that his children and the children of his playfellows may have such happy days open to them, too. Weather is a great transformer any time of the year. An earlier poet laureate noted boys rioting in a seven-inch snow on their way to school. " 'O look at the trees!' they cried, 'O look at the trees!' "[3]

Even when no snow has fallen, a walk to school or elsewhere through familiar streets can be a good time for looking and listening, stopping and examining. Making the rounds of yard or garden seldom fails to yield something new to the young child. If we are not pre-occupied, all of us can find something of fresh interest in everyday experience. But children, for whom so much remains to be revealed, are the most avid explorers of the immediate environment. When they

[2] William Wordsworth. "The Prelude." In: Thomas Hutchinson, editor. *The Poems of Wordsworth*. London: Oxford University Press, 1926. p. 636.

[3] John Greenleaf Whittier, "The Barefoot Boy"; John Betjeman, "Trebetherick"; and Robert Bridges, "London Snow."

are allowed to, they will make the most of things. Must they wait for June?

Moving Out

Always, the young adventurer feels the pull of going farther afield. Yonder—what will be found beyond the fence, down the street and around the corner, across the meadow, over the river and beyond the mountain? In our myth-making days, the far regions were populated by gods and monsters, and we loved to listen to the exploits of heroic travelers. Today the celebration of the urge and impulse of adventure has continued in fiction of many kinds.

In the lives of children, venturing into new territory proves both enticing and rewarding. It offers a quality of experience hard to equal. Yet venturesomeness has long been curtailed in the lives of many children. In her time, Margaret Fuller noted that when a woman tried to keep step with him, man was likely to be less than helpful:

> . . . [I]nstead of calling out like a good brother, "You can do it if you only think so," or impersonally, "Anyone can do what he tries to do," he often discourages with school-boy brag: "Girls can't do that. . . ."

Fuller urged union around the idea of a pervasive "creative energy" accessible to all. "Let it take what form it will, and let us not bind it by the past to man or woman, black or white."[4] A half century later another noted feminist was to put the message of "premature sex-consciousness" even more succinctly: "To the boy we say, 'Do'; to the girl, 'Don't.' "[5]

Tom Sawyer and his friends explored sandbars in the daytime, the cemetery at night, got lost in a cave—and, like Mark Twain himself, Huck Finn finally ran away downriver. Upon his return, finding Widow Perkins and her plot to civilize him too much to tolerate, Huck "lit out for the territory" beyond the settled towns. Mark Twain had preceded him after two and a half years on the river as apprentice and pilot—mining silver in Nevada, newspapering in San Francisco, spending a spell as special correspondent in the Sandwich Islands.

In fact and fiction, moving out is part of the American experience

---

[4] Margaret Fuller. "The Great Lawsuit." *The Dial* 4: 1-47; July 1843. Reprinted in: Alice S. Rossi, editor. *The Feminist Papers.* New York: Bantam Books, Inc., 1974. pp. 167, 180; punctuation modernized.

[5] Charlotte Perkins Gilman. *Women and Economics.* Boston, 1898. Reprinted in: *The Feminist Papers, op. cit.,* p. 578.

and always has been. Today we certainly get around more than any people ever did. Work-connected travel, change of job location, week-end and holiday and vacation travel—we are a mobile population, going everywhere and learning as we go. Yet venturesomeness within the school day, week, and year is strangely limited. A field trip or two each term, perhaps a week at camp for ten-year-olds, possibly an outdoor or land laboratory in the making, this seems to be about it.

Getting What They Can

Many new experiences come to children without being sought. Out and around on their own or along with older siblings or family adults, children may enter into a variety of unfamiliar environments where they do not know what there is to look for or learn about. Mahayag, a member of the stone age tribe discovered in the Philippines, was puzzled by questions about what the tribe would like to have from outside: "We don't know what we want because we cannot name things we don't know."[6]

For young children, much of their away-from-home experience would seem to be over their heads, so to speak. They hear a racket in the alley and catch a glimpse of an early morning nondomestic garbage raider. They find a "for sale" sign planted in the front yard where old Mrs. Montgomery lives, or lived. They watch a telephone worker climb a pole and call in. Such images and impressions, along with hunches and guesses, are stored away for reexamination and extension when the time comes. Young roamers have much to think about even though their thinking must remain intuitive. Distinctions between chance and order are beyond them at this point.[7]

All children, even infants, can profit from being included in adventures that are not fully meaningful at the time. A visit to a super-market, attendance at sports events, listening to and watching an open air concert, each leaves a residue of information and ideas in the mind of the child. Family events—visits to relatives, christenings, marriages, funerals perhaps—can be adventures into new realms. The same is true of public events, such as parades, election campaigns, state occasions, holiday observances. In brief, children do not have to get everything

[6] John Nance. *The Gentle Tasaday: A Stone Age People in the Philippine Rain Forest.* New York: Harcourt Brace Jovanovich, 1975. p. 154.

[7] Jean Piaget and Barbel Inhelder. *The Origin of the Idea of Chance in Children.* Translated by Lowell Leake and others. New York: W. W. Norton & Co., Inc., 1975.

that could be gotten from an experience for it to be worthwhile for them. Children learn what they can, and each adventure leaves a broader base for next time. Sometimes in school we may forget this in our desire to ensure orderly development.

Mapping the Territory

Young adventurers make the rounds, luxuriating in the privilege of being alive, and deepen as they can the satisfactions offered by their daily existence. They brave new regions of experience. They get all they can from the mysteries of the world that is opening up around them. And as they go, they lay out their maps. When Water Rat explains life aboveground to his new friend, the emancipated Mole, he describes the river and how it differs from season to season. He also identifies its demanding denizens—"'Otters, kingfishers, dabchicks, moorhens, all of them about all day long and always wanting you to *do* something'"— and charts the Wild Wood, with its squirrels and rabbits, weasels, stoats, and foxes. Ratty even disposes of the Wide World that lies beyond— "'Something that doesn't matter, either to you or me.'"[8]

Before he came to live for a while on its shore, Thoreau had visited Walden Pond almost daily for 20 years. A lake "is earth's eye; looking into which the beholder measures the depth of his own nature." But this beholder of Walden Pond had also walked around it, fished in it, boated on and swum in it, botanized it, taken its temperature and drunk its waters, and kept an eye on its water level. If he had been called upon to do so, Thoreau could have mapped the bottom of Walden Pond. He had measured its depths, as he had his own.[9]

In his 1740 adventure into the deep woods beyond the Delaware country, the young Natty Bumppo was stunned by his first sight of Lake Glimmerglass. A lake was something new to him, and

... he found a pleasure in studying this large and to him unusual opening into the mysteries and forms of the woods, as one is gratified in getting broader views of any subject that has occupied his thoughts.[10]

Much later, as an old trapper on the prairies, he could think back to his young maps with both amusement and regret. The land beyond the mountains was now all that was left to the true adventurer.

[8] Kenneth Grahame. *The Wind in the Willows.* New York: Avon Books, 1965. pp. 15-16.

[9] Henry David Thoreau. *Walden.* New York: Charles E. Merrill, 1910. p. 247.

[10] James Fenimore Cooper. *The Deerslayer.* New York: Macmillan Publishing Co., Inc., 1962. First published in Philadelphia in 1841.

First maps of any new world, as we know from history, are prone to error and always incomplete. A new river will be found later to run in another direction. Ponds will be relabeled lakes and lakes, seas. Some of the most distinctive features will have been overlooked. More mountains than deserts show up in the maps of young explorers.

Yet mapmaking is in our nature at every age. And the more expeditions we have been able to make into *terra incognita,* the more data we can draw on for guesses and hunches about what has happened or is happening to us. Adventuring will be thought a waste of time if or when we want instant accuracy in children. But if children are to have something to grow on, then we must not settle for anything less than the provision of as much lushness of environment as we can afford and as much leisure for children to explore this lushness as they can take (and we can tolerate).

Testing What They Learn

Confirmation or correction of what they think they are learning takes a fair share of every young adventurer's waking hours. In a story by Sherwood Anderson, an old writer becomes obsessed by a vision of mankind's earliest days. Then there were many vague thoughts but no truth. Finally, thoughts were combined to make truths—truths such as passion, wealth and poverty, thrift, carelessness and abandon. All these might have been good enough in themselves, but people tended to choose but one to live by. The truth thus became distorted, and people themselves turned into grotesques.[11] Reference to other persons and the realm of reality is essential if the truth is to become and remain whole. Being willing to put new insights to such a test is part of venturesomeness.

"Does this sort of thing happen often?" Surviving a rough time on the first of the hunts, their boat having capsized, Ishmael the novice whaler checks out his fears with shipmates. "Aye," Queequeg testifies. "Oh, yes," says Mr. Stubb. "Agreed," from Mr. Flask. So Ishmael retires below to make out his will.

Beautiful, rich, and a born adventuress, Daisy Miller insists on seeing the Colosseum by moonlight in the company of her admirer Giovanelli, with little regard for either reputation or health. Judged by her American compatriots to be ignorant if not common, Daisy had

[11] Sherwood Anderson. "The Book of the Grotesque." In: *Winesburg, Ohio.* New York: B. W. Huebsch, 1919.

checked out her learnings with the wrong set, ignoring the warnings of Mrs. Costello and the advice of wellwisher Winterbourne. Poor girl, she dies of a fever.

Confirmation or correction comes through the test of action, not merely from consultation with others. Ishmael is the sole survivor of Captain Ahab's madness, riding out the sinking of *The Pequod* on a coffin raft. "The unharming sharks, they glided by as if with padlocks on their mouths," he tells us; "the savage sea-hawks sailed with sheathed beaks." Unlike the ill-fated girl from Schenectady, Ishmael lived to tell the tale. But both had put their knowledge to the ultimate test.[12]

At all ages, adventurous learners look to others and to action for proof that they are making headway in the struggle to impose order on the miscellaneous items and events of experience. Freedom of interaction with the surrounding world maximizes the need for such tests. Children limited to studying the products of somebody else's adventuring do not have much call to put these to the test nor much occasion to try to push out the walls that pen them in.

In the child's world, undifferentiation yields only as there is more and more amplitude of interaction with objects. Accommodation to new possibilities of meaning comes when assimilation to old certainties ceases to make sense. These are Piaget's terms.[13] But the phenomena of natural learning through adventuring have long been understood by imaginative thinkers in every field of endeavor. "Slavery to self and slavery to the objective world are one and the same slavery."[14] What we all hope for are adventurous learners who will come through as adults in full charge of themselves.

A Framework for Change

"Man was born free, and everywhere he is in chains." In his first sentence, Rousseau put the chief paradox of an enlightened age plainly before the readers of *The Social Contract* (1762). For children, Blake would echo but alter this metaphor in "The Schoolboy" (1794):

12 Ishmael is, of course, the narrator of Herman Melville's *Moby Dick* (1851) and Daisy, the subject of *Daisy Miller* (1878) by Henry James.

13 See the concluding chapter, "The Elaboration of the Universe." In: Jean Piaget. *The Construction of Reality in the Child.* Margaret Cook, translator. New York: Basic Books, 1954.

14 Nicholas Berdyaev. *Slavery and Freedom.* R. M. French, translator. New York: Charles Scribner's Sons, 1944. p. 135.

How can the bird that is born for joy
Sit in a cage and sing?

Later, remarking on the dwindling of the woods around Walden Pond, Thoreau could ask: "How can you expect the birds to sing when their groves are cut down?" At the turn of the present century, Paul Laurence Dunbar could testify as to why some songs might still be sung. "I know why the caged bird sings!"[15] He was thinking of songs of desperation—pleas for freedom and prayers of escape.

Children are born free. And everywhere, if they are not in chains or cages, they find at least that their groves have been cut down or put out of bounds during school hours. When our children sing, it is all too often to mark the opening of another day of muted learning or to provide time-out from moving through their books.

Not all deterrents to adventuring originate in the schools. We have already noted this fact in identifying the children with whom our schools do least well. We must surely recognize the impact on children of restrictions in experience out of school as well as in (see Exhibit 5). As equalizer of opportunities for learning, we will accept these differences as part of the challenge. The point is that the range of adventuring for all children must be broadened, and how can this be done if not in school? As a kind of platform for action in this area, let us identify once again the elements that need to be combined in any effort to provide experiences that promote more intense interaction with an enriched environment for all children.

Adventuring as a Base for Learning

We have described learning through adventuring in terms of a number of somewhat general dimensions. Children learn as they make the most of whatever is around them. They move into new territory when they have a chance to learn what they can from it. In regions both familiar and unfamiliar, they begin to map what they think they know. And to be sure, they test their learning with other children and with adults as well as in more direct forms of action.

Can we specify what adventuring involves?

Interaction. Children must have opportunities to get together

[15] From: "Sympathy." In: Jay Martin and G. H. Hudson, editors. *The Complete Poems of Paul Laurence Dunbar.* New York: Dodd, Mead & Company, Inc., 1975. p. 316. Reprinted by permission.

Exhibit 5. Social Deterrents to Adventuring

Source of Restriction	Possible Impact on Children
Sex role	Some girls may be restricted to neighborhood or sex-related outings—shopping, visiting friends, etc.
	Some boys may come to regard use of cultural facilities—library, museums—as sissified.
Social class	Some working-class children may be uneasy about entering unfamiliar surroundings—downtown stores, library, museums, arboretum, etc.
	Some middle-class children may be uneasy about exploring less structured places—other neighborhoods, parks, open country, etc.
Income	Some children cannot afford transportation or other costs of more formal or elaborate outings.
Education	Some children may miss opportunities because parents do not know about or may undervalue available facilities—parks, museums, library, gardens, etc.
	Some children will lack home or private tutoring that would ready them to make the most of certain experiences—concerts, theater, etc.
Community	Children have fewer places to go in some communities—lack of natural or cultural facilities.
	Or they may find plenty of some kinds, not much of others; cities have some resources not found in small towns and rural areas—and vice versa.

with what is around them. Now and then we settle for playful exploration as the mode of learning. More often we talk of the need for hands-on activities, meaning the manipulation of objects or concrete materials, with the full use of all the senses. The mind has to be honored, too, for its controlling function in active learning as in any other kind of learning. The child interacts with environment to enjoy what is there but also to make sense out of it. The more sense, the greater the satisfaction: that is the open secret of why active learning works so well.

Options. Children must have some say in how to go about exploring a new environment. They need a chance to tie into it on their own terms. Prior learning and present interest will shape first responses. But children will be seeking something more, once the attraction of first choices dwindles. Children need to have a chance to change their minds —and thus options must be kept open all along the way. If adventuring is to remain alive and well, choice and change have to be kept in the picture.

Time. Children have to have time for exploring to get much out of it. A walk-through to sense the lay of the land may sometimes have value. But basking and plunging and basking again, scouring, leaping, and standing alone (vide Wordsworth) all take time. When we talk about making a place for adventuring, we are not thinking about in-between time, end-of-the-day time, time out or time off for good behavior, left-over time, or even free time. What we are thinking about is time that is reserved for immersion in an environment that absorbs attention and repays interaction. If it is to amount to anything as a base for learning, adventuring must bulk large in the daily and weekly schedule.

Nature of Environment

We have been using the term environment in several ways. After assaulting the immediate environment for sustenance, the infant soon begins to differentiate space beyond the breast or bottle to gain other kinds of satisfaction. An environment changes very quickly for the child as assimilation does its work and previously unnoticed features of familiar places insist on being accommodated. Making rounds of house and garden—or stoop and sidewalk—assures new learning. But altogether new environments are sought, too, by the active child. How big the world becomes!

Now we may find it useful to spell out a more explicit definition of a learning environment.

Variety. Children profit from having access to more than one environment. A change from one place to another breaks monotony. But more importantly it enables the lessons newly learned in one environment to be tested in another. When a strange environment becomes available, prior learnings are put to their severest test. How much of what I see do I already understand and know how to cope with? What remains to be explored? Where shall I begin? Challenge always comes as the scene for a child's experience changes.

Richness. Children interact with whatever is around them and thus the more to interact with, the better. No doubt there is a possibility of waste in a well-furnished environment. Yet children more often suffer from too little than too much. Constriction of the environment is a sure way to limit learning. Richness, while it does not guarantee learning, at least makes it possible. A wealth of resources—objects, materials, persons, other living things, events, features of terrain, and so on—must become of first concern as we select and develop environments for learning.

Size and space. Children need room to move around in if exploration is to come to much. The impact of constriction can be felt in cramped quarters as well as in too few resources. Unless they have the run of the place, children can hardly be expected to discover whatever there might be to discover. And of course standing still and simply looking around may be all that is possible when size and space confine rather than liberate the would-be adventurer. The crowded child is not likely to learn much.

Openness. Children stand to discover more of interest to them in relatively open surroundings than in those that are organized for specific uses. An arranged environment has its place on occasion. And some spaces have to be structured—instructional materials centers, gyms perhaps, and certain play areas. For the most part, however, environments that are explorable in more than one dimension serve the child adventurer best.

Experience: What Is It?

Adventuring in the right kind of environment provides worthwhile experiences. Some environments offer experiences that are good in themselves without too much teaching as such (see Exhibit 6). Whenever interaction with an environment endures for any length of time, it may be presumed to represent a search for sense as well as immediate satisfaction. Adventuring becomes formalized under such circumstances and leads to the kinds of experiences generally sponsored by the school.

Perhaps identifying the elements that go into organized experiences in adventuring will be useful at this point.

Purpose. Children need occasions for deciding what they wish to get from an adventure. Their immediate urges and impulses do well as a starting point but must be transformed into longer-term purposes if the search for satisfaction is to be sustained. While a series of sporadic raids upon new territory can be fun, in due time adventurers must take stock and think ahead. Otherwise, they may end up with not much more

Exhibit 6. Environments That May Offer Experiences Good in Themselves

Environments	Sample Experiences
1. *Topographical features*	Taking a bus trip into the country
Hill country	Walking around—uphill and down or across
Mountains	an open field
Wooded areas	Watching to see what the waves bring in
Fields and meadows	
Desert	
Swamps	
Streams and rivers	
Ponds and lakes	
Seashore	
2. *Parks*	Visiting a forest of redwoods or other giant trees
Forests	
Contrasting habitats	Following a trail to look at wildflowers
Nature trails: wild flowers, trees, birds, animals	
Exhibits	
Workshops and laboratories	
3. *Recreational areas*	Taking a boat ride
Ponds for fishing and boating	Cooking lunch after a morning hike
Swimming pool	Going swimming or playing baseball
Tennis courts	
Baseball diamond	
Hiking and bike trails	
Picnicking facilities: water, fireplaces, tables	
4. *Government agencies and offices*	Touring the statehouse
City hall	Visiting a firehouse, examining equipment, and talking with a firefighter
Statehouse	
Post office	Visiting the post office
Courts	
Firehouse	
Police station	
5. *Cultural institutions*	Listening to a story in the children's department of the public library
Schools	
Colleges	Attending a performance of *The Nutcracker Suite*
Libraries	
Museums: art, science and industry, historical	Visiting herb garden, tasting bits of herbs
Arboretum	
Gardens	
Theaters	

Environments	Sample Experiences
6. *Merchandising centers* Supermarkets Produce market Shopping malls Downtown department stores Village main street	Looking for unfamiliar fruits and vegetables in a market Walking through a new mall
7. *Work sites* Factories Warehouses Greenhouses Farms Dairies TV studios Publishing: newspapers, books Workshops: arts and crafts	Seeing videotape equipment in action at a TV studio Buying plants for school at a greenhouse or nursery Watching artisans in a cooperative workshop: pottery, leather work, etc.
8. *Transportation* Bus station Railway station Airport Ports and harbors Highway system State traffic control	Touring the airport Going for a boat ride around the harbor or down the river
9., *Neighborhoods* Old section Restored section Apartment areas Suburbs: old, new Estates	Walking along streets and visiting shops in Old Town or German Village Inspecting a new apartment development with adult and young family areas
10. *Towns, cities, and open country* Roads and highways Housing Population: density Occupations	Visiting a village with stops at general store, bakery, health center, farm machinery salesroom, etc. Touring the downtown section of a city

than a head full of images and impressions. Mining and mapping call for a definition of ends beforehand. What are we after? Where do we want to go?

Exercise of powers. Children must have focused opportunities to develop and strengthen their natural powers—getting the lay of the land, finding out something, handling their bodies, expressing their thoughts, responding to the ideas of others, making something, working together, and so on. A good experience in adventuring or in any other approach to learning will keep the exercise of these powers in the foreground. In the process of using their powers, children reach out for the facts and skills they need to be increasingly effective.

Outcome. After a good experience has been completed, children will have something to hold to. Sometimes it is a vivid memory, sometimes a sharpened awareness. More often we would anticipate the emergence of new insights to be tested—the interrelationship of life forms, contrasts between small-town and urban living, the varied functions of a museum; or the creation of a product of some kind to be shared—a chart or a graph, a poem or a painting, a boat or a tin of muffins. In any case, the experience has left something behind that provides a broader base to build on or a higher elevation from which to take the next flight.

Extensions of Content: Some Possibilities

Do we mean business about developing a new curriculum for children? If so, we must agree that we could find no better place to begin than in the realm of adventuring.

All over America on a Monday morning children stir and murmur against the closing in of school routine. By 9:15 a.m. some of them, their eyes out of focus, begin to yawn. Their pencils loosen in their fists. As they bend over to pick them up, children may come alive again and turn to the task at hand. Copy . . . fill in . . . write . . . complete . . . hand in. Somehow by Tuesday children are back in harness, doing what does not come naturally. But by Friday! What a day Friday can be for young ones, who can hardly wait to be let out for the weekend—and for their keepers, too, who can hardly wait to let them go.

When they come to us, children have already had a lifetime of learning based on what comes naturally. In plain and simple terms, our challenge is to sustain the exploratory urge and impulse that exists in all children. To do so we must gain a better grasp of what really counts in the strengthening of natural powers. Once we accept the need for adventuring as a base for much learning, we should be able to identify the environments that most deserve to be explored. To make full use of these, we must arrange for authentic interaction, choice among approaches, and plenty of time for it all.

Our intention is to call into play all the capacities of all our children as much of the time as possible Monday through Friday. The achievement of worthwhile outcomes is to become their goal as well as ours. Partnership in setting purposes is where we have to start.

Exploration of the Natural Environment

Today many forces support school sponsorship of an expanded program of outdoor experiences for children and youth. Sports persons, wildlife and wilderness buffs, back-to-nature enthusiasts, old-line nature lovers and conservationists, the new antipollution political activists, park and recreation personnel, and ecologists from the several life sciences— all agree that the young will profit from spending more time in guided exploration of their natural environment. Reconciling the diverse interests and concerns of these groups may be difficult. But what power there is in their combined know-how and zeal!

Ecological studies. The last known passenger pigeon, housed in the Cincinnati zoo, died in 1914. Less than a century earlier, in the vicinity of Louisville, Audubon had noted the beginning of a three-day migration of the birds southward across the Ohio River. "The air was literally filled with pigeons that obscured the light of noonday like an eclipse."[16] Today ecological disaster comes quicker. Moving at the rate of a mile every ten days, an 82-ton dragline in no time at all can eat up a river and drain a swamp. And it may be doing so under orders of the Soil Conservation Service of the U.S. Department of Agriculture.[17] The otters and alligators do not have a say in the matter. Nor, we may feel, do most of us.

As tomorrow's voters, children need to know more than their parents about relationships among living things and between living things and their habitat. Otherwise, people may become an endangered species. At this point, our goal is clearer than our immediate objectives. What is called for is something more than touching children's hearts with the plight of pelicans and polar bears or enlisting their energies in a neighborhood cleanup campaign. Good though these ends and activities may be, they are hardly enough. A greater intimacy between the young and their natural environment would seem to be where we must

16 John James Audubon. In: Alice Ford, editor. *Audubon, by Himself.* New York: Thomas Y. Crowell Company, 1969. p. 70.

17 John McPhee. "Travels in Georgia." In: *Pieces of the Frame.* New York: Farrar, Straus, and Giroux, Inc., 1975. pp. 3-60.

start. If we have this to build on, perhaps we can trust that in time specific purposes and outcomes will come clear.

Other field studies. "Nature and the earth should be equivalent terms, and so should earth study and nature study."[18] This is Dewey talking about the need to relate science and geography. Adventuring into the natural environment can certainly provide experiences in more areas than ecology. Topography comes to life when children trudge up a hillside or slide down a grassy slope. Geology means something to young scientists armed with hammers and specimen bags and headed for an abandoned quarry. Archaeology, though it remain unnamed, may add another dimension to adventuring when children dig around in the dump heap of an abandoned farm or locate and pace off the crumbling foundations of its house and outbuildings.

While some field studies may be formalized, other forays may be allowed to run their course as minor or modest ventures in sensing or sizing up the possibilities of a given environment. A new supply of images and impressions may be yield enough for a half day spent in roaming a wooded area or tracing a rivulet through field and meadow.

Attention to landscape. Experiences with a variety of landscapes, natural and managed, can alert adventurers of any age to relationships among land forms, vegetation, water, space, structures, pathways, and other elements that combine to make a prospect pleasing.[19] Looking closely at landscapes of different elevations may highlight problems of emphasis and balance. Study of managed environments will reveal radical differences in the role given to grass, gardens, landshaping, and the like.

Offering children many opportunities to respond to the landscape in aesthetic terms hardly needs justification. Such experiences become more deliberately purposeful as children identify elements and principles of composition and design. These may be used to describe and compare landscapes and eventually to design or redesign vistas. Carrying through on school, home, or neighborhood planting projects can put knowledge to the test.

Outdoor recreation. The natural environment excels in variety, richness, size and space, and openness. And perhaps no other environ-

[18] John Dewey. *Democracy and Education.* New York: Macmillan Publishing Co., Inc., 1916. p. 250.

[19] See: Nan Fairbrother. *The Nature of Landscape Design: As an Art Form, a Craft, a Social Necessity.* New York: Alfred A. Knopf, Inc., 1974.

ment invites such a range of interactions, among the most intense of which are the pursuits we label recreational. As we have noted, the self-selected summer activities of the young set a high standard for planned adventuring.

Swimming, fishing, boating, camping, hiking, climbing, and all the rest—these are good-in-themselves experiences that also build a broad base for learning in other areas. In the late 1860's, Mark Twain and companions from Canyon City camped for two or three weeks on the north shore of Lake Tahoe. For these adventurers, who saw no other persons during their stay, each day was a new experience. The play of wind and weather, the changing forest vistas glimpsed from a drifting boat, the glittering snow and landslide scars on the circling mountains, "and now and then the far-off thunder of an avalanche" combined to educate or reeducate their senses. "The eye was never tired of gazing, night or day, in calm or storm; it suffered but one grief, and that was that it could not look always but must close sometimes in sleep." [20]

Adventuring, we may agree, should be extended to embrace outdoor recreation. And with the school as sponsor, it need not be confined to a single season. Ecological and other field studies and attention to the landscape will change their shape as the seasons change, and so it is with recreation.

Our case for thinking seriously of the possibility of doing more with exploring the natural environment in an equal rights curriculum for children is easy to review:

Adventuring here as elsewhere is hard to beat as a way of learning whatever there is that can be learned. Are children ever more alive, joyful, interested, active, and at peace with themselves and others than in these circumstances?[21] Adventuring in the world of nature can contribute to learning in many areas of academic concern.

In particular, such adventuring is needed as a base for understanding what it takes to sustain and enrich life in all its forms.

And adventuring of this kind often offers experiences that are just plain good in themselves.

[20] Mark Twain. *Roughing It.* New York: Harper and Brothers, 1959. p. 161. First published 1871.

[21] The qualities we cite are those named by Fromm as belonging to the character structure of life-oriented persons. See: Erich Fromm. *The Revolution of Hope: Toward a Humanistic Technology.* New York: Bantam Books, Inc., 1968. p. 94.

Today some children have more chances than others to enjoy and learn from adventures in the world of nature, but few children have as many as they might find profitable. We are already moving to do more for children in environmental education. Can we broaden our approach—and step it up?

Exploring the Built Environment

As he watched the high surf climb the beach below his tower at Carmel and relieve it of summer's litter, the poet Robinson Jeffers had a vision that we may sometimes be inclined to share. Could such a surf rise even higher, it might cleanse the entire continent. "The cities gone down, the people fewer and the hawks more numerous," then man might "regain the dignity of room, the value of rareness."[22] No doubt we can adapt to high-density living, but at what expense? The danger is not so much that man will crowd himself to death "but that he will learn to live with his fellow men only too well."[23]

Public decisions about where people should live, where they should work, and where shared facilities should be located are being made today with little awareness of or concern for planning and design principles.[24] All of us, adults as well as children, have much to learn from a more conscious exploration of the built environment.

Study of neighborhoods. "At one time people had cared about these houses," James Baldwin's Vivaldo muses as he passes along Harlem's Lenox Avenue. Once the neighborhood had "been home, whereas now it was a prison."[25] In a sense, any neighborhood can have walls around it. The child of the ghetto may grow up resigned as well as bitter. The child of the suburbs may grow up not so much unconcerned as simply unaware.

Neighborhoods differ, and seeing that this is so must be part of any study of where people live. Under our guidance, children may begin to wonder how some areas survive and why. Can we also hope to help children look at what people need in any good neighborhood? And why

[22] Robinson Jeffers. "November Surf." In: *Thurso's Landing and Other Poems.* New York: Liveright Publishing Corporation, 1932. p. 128.

[23] J. Charles Mercer. "Toward Standing Room Only." In: David Carter and Terence Lee, editors. *Psychology and the Built Environment.* London: The Architectural Press, Ltd., 1974; and New York: John Wiley & Sons, Inc., 1974. p. 199.

[24] See: R. Fraser Reekie. *Design in the Built Environment.* New York: Crane, Russak, 1972. pp. 60-62.

[25] James Baldwin. *Another Country.* New York: The Dial Press, Inc., 1962. p. 114.

it is, that when free to choose, some families prefer apartment living to home ownership, some the small town to the city? And what good neighborhoods of the future might be like?

Futurism and forecasting in environmental reconstruction, while they have their perils, can reveal new possibilities and even new values. Perhaps with children the challenge is to join the need to adventure ahead of ourselves in this field with the pleasure it brings. "Seeking closure and certainty is human enough," one distinguished urban planner remarks. "But so is the joy of creation, of breaking out." [26]

Work sites: where and why. Many forces operate to bring different neighborhoods into being. Similarly, people congregate for good reason at a variety of work sites—"the shop, yard, store, or factory" of Whitman's "A Song for Occupations":

> These shows all near you by day and night—workman! whoever you
> are, your daily life! [27]

The poet urges "the workwomen and workmen of these States" to look for "the best, or as good as the best" in the things around them.

Many school children do get chances to explore some aspects of the work environment. They may visit a dairy, a supermarket warehouse, a newspaper plant. With the current emphasis on career education, other avenues of exploration may be opening up.

But the place of work sites in the built environment cannot be perceived in such a piecemeal approach. The downtown office towers serviced by workers who live close at hand, the abandoned railway yards, the score of great shopping malls that form new towns around the city, the industrial parks that line the newly completed outerbelt—these are the sites to which attention must be paid if choice is to come alive. Adventure here, to be sure, is a matter of partnership between child and adult. We are all in this together.

Shared facilities. Government buildings, parks and playgrounds, streets and highways, schools, libraries—each community differs in what it offers along these lines. In one town, political rallies may be held in the Veterans' Memorial Auditorium, dedicated in 1920; in another, in the sports arena of an as yet unfinished convention center. But the functions remain the same. Shared facilities celebrate community.

[26] Kevin Lynch. *What Time Is This Place?* Cambridge, Massachusetts: M.I.T. Press, 1972. pp. 101-102.

[27] Walt Whitman, *op. cit.,* p. 187.

Moreover, they endure longer than most structures. The courthouse is less likely than any other building in the county seat to be torn down. As they study what we have been willing to spend tax money on, children can see where we have been. "All architecture," Whitman points out to his "dear scholars," the common folk, "is what you do to it when you look upon it."

Probably the prime example of the impact of public planning upon the built environment is to be found in the highway system. Dramatic change has taken place in almost every community and often within the lifetime of quite young children. And change continues, making observation of the now and the then and the yet-to-be possible from vantage points everywhere along the throughways that skirt our towns and cities and race on to remake the American countryside.

The built environment is varied, rich, large in size and scope, and open to countless kinds of interaction by children. The purposes to be developed for its study can arise from and be related to many conventional content areas. The pursuit of these purposes can call for exercise of the full range of children's powers.

And here as in study of the natural environment, the outcome of such experiences is of critical importance if the concept of equal rights is to mean as much outside of school as we hope it will within. Neighborhoods and work sites and shared facilities, different as they are, can often be altered to be better for everybody concerned.

Of even larger interest is the relationship between natural and built environments. The need to contain the size of urban areas and stop denaturalizing them has been called to our attention by many planners.[28] But it is only as we come to understand and love the claims of both that we can act with intelligence.

The kind of study adventures we are proposing should help in realizing new ends in our built environment. Can we commit ourselves to move on in doing more with this aspect of children's education?

Adventures in the Cultural Realm

"I wish you could go through this section of our common country and speak to them trumpet-tongued on the great theme," wrote the young Henry Barnard to his Massachusetts mentor. He was reporting

---

[28] As, for example, by: J. J. Shomon. *Open Land for Urban America*. Baltimore: Johns Hopkins Press, 1971.

from Louisville in the winter of 1843 on what he had learned from a speaking tour that had taken him also into Ohio and Michigan. "It is sad to look around on the evidences of deficient and perverted education, and think of the ransomless state of ignorance into which so many of these children are sold by the miserable demagogues who abound in these western legislatures." [29] His correspondent, of course, was Horace Mann.

The struggle for support of the common schools has long since been won. All our children are in school, as we have noted. But a visitor of today's western and other regions may still be of a mind to use strong language about our neglect of many children. How little we do, it may seem to some, to help children transcend the limitations of their out-of-school experience. In no area is this more apparent, many might contend, than in what we may call the cultural realm, in which evidences of deficiency and ignorance and perversion of purpose lie all about us.

The arts as environment. "The first sentiment of an uncorrupted mind, when it enters upon the theatre of human life is, Remove from me and my fellows all arbitrary hindrances: let us start fair." So wrote the great expounder on political justice, William Godwin, in 1795. "Education should enable us to meet any free circumstance with a sporting chance of success." [30] This latter call for equal opportunity comes from the distinguished contemporary musician, Yehudi Menuhin.

Yet children still do not start fair nor have a sporting chance in gaining full access to the arts. In music, as the composer Ned Rorem reminds us, we "hear all music by comparing it to all the other music" we have known. When we have not heard much then "our experience is clearly narrow." [31]

The realm of music into which children can adventure is rich and far reaching—old music and new, eastern and western music, music that is serious and popular music in all its variety. Part of the excitement of the arts is finding uniquenesses to respond to. "We want different contents and different forms," LeRoi Jones contends, in arguing for the

[29] Vincent P. Lannie, editor. *Henry Barnard: American Educator.* New York: Teachers College Press, 1974. p. 83.

[30] Yehudi Menuhin. *Theme and Variations.* New York: Stein and Day, 1972. p. 82. Copyright © 1972 by Yehudi Menuhin. Reprinted by permission of Stein and Day.

[31] Ned Rorem. *Pure Contraption: A Composer's Essays.* New York: Holt, Rinehart and Winston, Inc., 1974. p. 140. Copyright © 1974 by Ned Rorem. Reprinted by permission.

need to honor black music, with its base in rhythm and blues, "because we have different feelings. We are a different people." [32]

We have used music to make our case. We could say much the same about the graphic arts, theater, the dance, and so on. A great deal more is available in the arts environment, both at first hand and in recordings, prints, films, and TV programs, than we have cared to take into account in working with children.

History: dead and alive. Another dimension of the cultural realm that invites and rewards children's adventuring is history. "There was history all around us, indeed," recalls a journalist in thinking over his schooling in Laramie, Wyoming, about 1910, "but it had not got into the textbooks yet, and to my recollection no teacher thought of fitting it into the curriculum." Close at hand were traces of the Overland Trail, sites of Indian battles, and much more. Now Laramie was inhabited mostly by North Europeans who had come late. Geography could have begun with the personal testimony of elders in families like the Berglunds, the Johnsons, the Olsons. [33]

Every community has historical sites to explore, oldtimers to talk to, old parts of town to take a look at. Museums and private collections of artifacts are often located just around the corner. A short day's trip will take most children to the state capitol and home again. More extensive adventures can be highly enlightening to older children: a slip back into the past to find out how we lit our homes, prepared and preserved our food, made our clothing, got to church and back; where we have been in farming, road building, water management; sites of old conflicts and catastrophes, such as battles and floods and hurricanes, and places where enduring concerns are still pursued—Indian reservations, for example, or institutions for those who may need to be cared for or kept apart.

The intellectual community. Some children are born into a family or social unit whose members have freed themselves from the burden of undue "admiration of antiquity, authority, and unanimity," to use Francis Bacon's words. In the mid-1830's, select children were privileged to attend the Temple School in Boston, where Bronson Alcott, sometimes called the American Pestalozzi, led them in conversations

[32] LeRoi Jones. "The Changing Same: R & B and New Black Music." In: *Black Music.* New York: William Morrow and Company, Inc., 1967. Reprinted by permission of The Sterling Lord Agency.

[33] Ted Olson. *Ranch on the Laramie.* Boston: Little, Brown and Company, 1973. p. 48.

based on readings from the New Testament and from literary "Works of Genius," inspiring efforts at self-analysis and reasoning on conduct that were dutifully confided to open journals.[34] From 1836 to 1840, Alcott was a member of the Transcendental Club, of which Emerson was the leading light. "In some form," Emerson noted, "the question comes to each: Will you fulfill the demands of the soul, or will you yield to the conventions of the world?" ("Human Life," 1838). That was the question then, to be pondered by Margaret Fuller, Henry David Thoreau, and Theodore Parker, along with other members of the club. And it is the question now; it is always the question of the intellectual community.

Entry into this community ought to be open to every child, not confined to a fortunate few. Certainly today more children than in the time of Alcott and Emerson enter adulthood with "the capacity to see new things," a power identified by the anthropologist as basic to needed culture change.[35] Yet too many children never adventure very far into the realm of conscious concern for what is at war with the human spirit in their surroundings and what they might do about it. We have miles to go—and promises to keep.

Our cultural environment—the realm of the arts, history, and critical self-awareness—is as expansive and perhaps as much neglected as our natural and built environments. Adventures in interacting with it deeply and freely demand more time than we have thought we had to spare from what we have considered to count for most.

But where else can we hope for such a payoff? We are dealing here with the essence of the common heritage, hitherto hidden away from a good part of the human race and possibly less accessible than it might have been to all our children.

Are we ready to open the gates?

Summary and Conclusion

Can we do more with adventuring as a base for learning?

We are not thinking here of simply turning children out upon the community. As we are set up now, an increase in interaction with the

---

[34] Dorothy McCuskey. *Bronson Alcott, Teacher.* New York: Macmillan Publishing Company, Inc., 1940. Chapter 5, "The Temple School."

[35] Margaret Mead and Frances G. Macgregor. *Growth and Culture: A Photographic Study of Balinese Childhood.* Based upon photographs by: Gregory Bateson. New York: G. P. Putnam's Sons, 1951. Chapter 1, "The Need for Awareness."

natural, built, and cultural environments where we live will call for a great deal of planning ahead. The claims of the selected environments we have been describing will have to be examined closely in terms of ease of interaction and openness of options as well as time management (see Exhibit 7). Some of us may want to quarrel over the presumed ends to be achieved socially as well as intellectually through the exploration of these environments.

But can there be any doubt that a return to the home base of adventuring with children could give us promise of a new start with many children for whom school as it is does not seem to take hold?

Exhibit 7. Adventuring in Selected Environments: Some Comparisons

Criteria for Adventuring	Natural	Built	Cultural
Ease of interaction: accessibility	All about us, even in the city, but obviously more varied in suburbs and rural regions	Inescapable for most children today although small town and rural children will have to have help in reaching a variety of neighborhoods and work sites	Everywhere at hand as far as history goes; the arts may be mostly second-hand (recordings, TV, etc.); the intellectual community may be confined to print for most children
Openness of options: absence of structure	Nonstructured by definition; differences in features (water, trees, elevation) will impose some limitations	Developed areas likely to be found apart in terms of function—residential, work, governmental—especially in larger communities	What is there open to free choice; limitation comes from lack of richness and variety
Time management: flexibility	Has to be arranged for in advance	Except for school neighborhood, has to be arranged for	May be on call as far as secondhand resources are concerned (books, prints, recordings, etc.); persons and sites for history study have to be arranged for as would attending concerts, exhibits, and so on

We are calling for a broadened and more life-oriented base for learning—a more varied, richer, larger, and more open arena.

We are asking for children to have a chance to frame good reasons for learning from interaction with selected environments.

We are claiming that in the pursuit of such purposes children will be able to bring their natural or personal powers into fuller play.

We are urging the prospect that experiences of this kind will have outcomes for many previously poorly taught children that will put them far ahead of the game compared to schooling in the past.

We must admit that we think adventuring in these realms will be good for just about all children—and for society, too.

Maybe that is enough to argue for. And of course it is not all that is to be attempted in developing a new curriculum. Let us move along.

Mastering

As they get out and around in the world, children come to know how much there is to know. And if their explorations are broadly based, they learn a lot of what they need to learn—about the shape and size of things, the conditions of the good life, the responsiveness of selected environments to those who are aware of possibilities and able to act on them. That is what adventuring has to offer. Every child deserves a chance to come alive—or at least to stay awake!—during school hours.

What Has To Be Done

But adventuring into the world is not enough. Mastering it—that is what counts. Children become increasingly competent in handling themselves as they have many opportunities to dig in and do what they must to make the world their own.

Impelled by the drive to find satisfaction in their experience, children put all their powers to work full force on wresting from the world whatever it has to offer. As they grow in mastery of their circumstances, they begin to be able to make increasing sense out of what is happening. Choices, better informed and thus wiser, are more rewarding. Mastering the world has many aims and pays off in all directions. (See Exhibit 8 for a relevant vocabulary.) "I am the Unacknowledged Champion of

Everything!" the child, like Nelson Algren's celebrator of the spring-time, might seem to be saying. And the world—what is it? "The garden where all things are possible."[1]

Exhibit 8. A Vocabulary of Mastering: Aims and Dimensions

accomplishing	dominating	mastering	resolving
achieving	excelling	maturing	solving
acquiring	finishing	overcoming	subduing
advancing	gaining	passing	succeeding
attaining	getting	perfecting	surmounting
beating	governing	persevering	transcending
besting	grasping	persisting	triumphing
completing	improving	possessing	vanquishing
controlling	laboring over	prevailing	winning
conquering	learning	pursuing	
developing	managing	reaching	

Not without hard work, however. The stream of life brings with it something new every day. "Life itself is the effort of the organism to cope continually with the ever oncoming novelty." These are the words of William Heard Kilpatrick. "The true unit of study is the organism-in-its-interaction-with-the-environment."[2] And to make sure that this encounter leads to mastery takes some doing, both by children and teacher.

Survival may not sound like much of an ambition, but for some children it represents a triumph over circumstances difficult to endure and impossible to control. Dealing with life outside of school may be reduced to learning to hold on. Even in favored circumstances, a surplus of adult control may constrict the free play of children's powers and purposes. But when they come to school, children ought to be able to move into areas where mastering is open to all. That is our challenge.

How can the drive toward mastering best be sustained? What matters most in the exercise and strengthening of personal powers in this arena? Which sets of competencies are most worthy of school sponsorship? Answers to these questions will make sense only as we

---

[1] Nelson Algren. "The Ryebread Trees of Spring." In: *The Last Carousel*. New York: G. P. Putnam's Sons, 1973. p. 256.

[2] William H. Kilpatrick. *Remaking the Curriculum*. New York: Newsom and Company, 1936. p. 116.

keep in mind what has to be done in mastering anything. Free to do so, children are eager to get on with the task of making the world their own.

Taking It On

When his new friend Fosdick, orphaned but educated, undertook to be his tutor, Dick the bootblack had almost everything to learn.

But if Dick was ignorant, he was quick, and had an excellent capacity. Moreover he has perseverance, and was not easily discouraged. He had made up his mind he must know more, and was not disposed to complain of the difficulty of his task. Fosdick had occasion to laugh more than once at his ludicrous mistakes; but Dick laughed too, and on the whole both were quite interested in the lesson.

At the end of an hour and a half the boys stopped for the evening.

"You're learning fast, Dick," said Fosdick. "At this rate you will soon learn to read well."

"Will I?" asked Dick with an expression of satisfaction. "I'm glad of that. I don't want to be ignorant. I didn't use to care, but I do now. I want to grow up 'spectable."

Dick studied every night and before a year was out had made great strides in his learning.

He could now read well, write a fair hand, and had studied arithmetic as far as Interest. Besides this he had obtained some knowledge of grammar and geography.

Boy readers of *Ragged Dick; or Street Life in New York* (1870) were urged by its author, if they wondered at such progress, to remember that "our hero was very much in earnest in his desire to improve" and was "determined to make the most of himself—a resolution which is the secret of success in nine cases out of ten." [3]

When she was eleven, Elizabeth Cady Stanton (1815-1902) resolved to comfort her father and compensate for the death of her beloved only brother by becoming what he had been.

I thought that the chief thing to be done in order to equal boys was to be learned and courageous. So I decided to study Greek and learn to manage a horse.

She "learned to leap a fence and ditch on horseback" and "began to study Latin, Greek, and mathematics with a class of boys at the

[3] Horatio Alger. *Struggling Upward and Other Works.* New York: Crown Publishers, Inc., 1945. pp. 225-26, 246. Copyright © 1945, 1973 by Crown Publishers, Inc. Reprinted by permission.

Academy, many of whom were older than I." After three years, she won a prize in Greek.

> One thought alone filled my mind. "Now," said I, "my father will be satisfied with me."
>
> I rushed breathless into his office, laid the new Greek Testament, which was my prize, on his table and exclaimed: "There, I got it!" He took up the book, asked me some questions about the class, and, evidently pleased, handed it back to me. Then he kissed me on the forehead and exclaimed, with a sigh, "Ah, you should have been a boy!" [4]

Disappointed she may have been. But, at the Academy and in her father's law office, the founder-to-be of the woman suffrage movement got a good start on a lifetime of purposeful learning.

Street boy or lawyer's daughter, girl or boy—the invitation to master what there is to know should be open to each and all. "The world is as new to him as it was to the first man that existed," Thomas Paine declared in exalting the claims of the free-born child, "and his natural right in it is of the same kind" (*Rights of Man,* 1791). Fact, fiction, and philosophy come together here.

Finding a Way

In Philadelphia in the late 1720's, young Ben Franklin borrowed books overnight from booksellers' apprentices as he sought to extend his acquaintance with the world's great literature. A century later in Baltimore, Frederick Douglass (1817-1895), who had been taught the first steps of reading by his owner's wife, Miss Sophie, got his subsequent lessons on the run from white playfellows. *Webster's Spelling Book* was always in his pocket. When everyone else slept, he read the great speeches in *The Columbian Orator,* purchased for 50 cents, or the hymns in the Methodist hymnbook or another chapter from the Bible.[5] Like many others of the era, Abe Lincoln also learned to read and write mostly on his own.

The tomboy of the March family hid out as she scribbled her way toward proficiency and publication.

[4] Elizabeth Cady Stanton. "Excerpts from Her Autobiography." In: Eve Merriam, editor. *Growing Up Female in America.* New York: Doubleday & Company, Inc., 1971. pp. 54-55. Copyright © 1971 by Eve Merriam. Reprinted by permission of Doubleday & Company, Inc.

[5] Frederick Douglass. *Life and Times of Frederick Douglass: His Early Life as a Slave, His Escape from Bondage, and His Complete History, Written by Himself.* New York: Collier Books, 1962; first published 1892.

Jo was very busy in the garret, for the October days began to grow chilly, and the afternoons were short. For two or three hours the sun lay warmly in the high window, showing Jo seated on the old sofa, writing busily . . . till the last page was filled, when she signed her name with a flourish, and threw down her pen, exclaiming, —

"There, I've done my best! If this won't suit I shall have to wait till I can do better." [6]

A generation earlier the lonely children in the parsonage at Haworth had transformed themselves into a colony of romance writers. Charlotte herself had turned out 23 "novels" in a little more than a year's time.

Genius finds a way to master circumstances, come what may. Is that our point? We would prefer to join Piaget in contending that intelligence is not "an independent absolute but is a relationship . . . between the organism and things." [7] When interaction between child and environment is fully supportive in school or out, control increases. In the process, the child's native powers, of which Caleb Gattegno speaks so movingly, are exercised and developed. [8] Perhaps we do need to learn how to "energize" the child, to use the language of William James, [9] or to "activitate" him "so that he can experience his own capacity to solve problems and have enough success so that he can feel rewarded for the exercise of thinking." [10]

Or we may decide that it is sounder to do less in order to do more. "Help me to help myself." That is the child's cry from the heart, hard for us to hear and harder yet to heed. If we are trying to honor "the creative impulses" of the child, how careful we must be, Doctor Montessori reminds us, not to cross "the threshold of intervention" too soon. [11]

Staying the Course

Mastering is the process by which children make the world their own. They take on the confusion around them, "the initial phase of all

[6] Louisa M. Alcott. *Little Women.* 1868. Chapter 14, "Secrets."

[7] Jean Piaget. *The Origins of Intelligence in Children.* Margaret Cook, translator. New York: W. W. Norton & Company, Inc., 1963. p. 19.

[8] Caleb Gattegno. *What We Owe Children: The Subordination of Teaching to Learning.* New York: Outerbridge, 1970. Chapter 1, "The Powers of Children."

[9] William James. *Selected Papers in Philosophy.* New York: E. P. Dutton & Co., Inc., 1917. "The Energies of Man." pp. 40-57.

[10] Jerome S. Bruner. *The Relevance of Education.* New York: W. W. Norton & Company, Inc., 1971. p. 71.

[11] Maria Montessori. *The Child in the Family.* Nancy R. Cirillo, translator. Chicago: Henry Regnery Company, 1970. p. 116.

knowledge, without which one cannot progress to clarity." [12]   They find a way to work out their puzzlement—or many ways. "There is no route map of the way to truth," Franz Kafka observed. "The only thing that counts is to make the venture of total dedication." [13]   In his old age, the passionate sightseer Bernard Berenson paid 20 visits to an exhibit of illuminated manuscripts in Venice, noting in his journal that it would take a lifetime to master them. All we have time for on earth, he had long since concluded, is "to decide what topics we should pursue if we had eternity at our disposal." [14]

Dedication to the pursuit of mastery is to be taken for granted in the living and learning of children. How often the bike is righted and remounted, how often the ball is bounced and the basket aimed for, how many tries before a new paddler makes it across the pool and back! A fifth-grade science project, like Coker Ray Gibson's on spiders, can go much beyond what we expect. Mrs. Markas was not sure that so much about spiders would be welcomed when time for sharing came. (Poor troubled Coker had a problem larger than that: he didn't know if he should turn his black widows loose in his tormented mother's room— or his own.) [15]

The career of astronomer Maria Mitchell (1818-1889) began as she aided her father in making observations from the rooftop of their island home. "In Nantucket," she later testified, "people generally are in the habit of observing the heavens, and a sextant will be found in almost every house." For 20 years after leaving school at 16 she studied on her own, winning a gold medal from the King of Denmark for discovering a comet and being elected the first woman member of the American Academy of Arts and Sciences (1848). Then as professor of astronomy and director of the observatory at Vassar College, she joined teaching to her continuing studies. "The world of learning is so broad," she noted in her diary in 1854, "and the human soul is so limited in power." [16]

12 José Ortega y Gasset. *The Origin of Philosophy.* Toby Talbot, translator. New York: W. W. Norton & Company, Inc., 1967. p. 52.

13 Gustav Janouch. *Conversations with Kafka.* G. Rees, translator. New York: New Directions Press, 1971. p. 156. Copyright © 1968, 1971 by Fischer Verlag. Reprinted by permission of New Directions Publishing Corporation.

14 Bernard Berenson. *The Passionate Sightseer.* From the Diaries, 1947 to 1956. New York: Harry Abrams, Inc., 1960. p. 36.

15 Doris Betts. "The Spider Gardens of Madagascar." In: *Beasts of the Southern Wild and Other Stories.* New York: Harper & Row, Publishers, 1973. pp. 133-52.

16 Maria Mitchell. "Extracts from Her Diary." In: *Growing Up Female in America, op. cit.,* pp. 75, 80.

Berenson and Mitchell and all of us as strivers after knowledge, young and old, then and now—it is in our nature to want to know and also to discover that we can never learn enough. "We never pursue things—it is the pursuit itself that we enjoy," Pascal proposed. "Only the struggle pleases us, we are not concerned for victory" (*Pensee* 132). Or as Camus expressed it: "Any fulfillment is a bondage. It obliges one to a higher fulfillment."[17]

Minding Their Own Business

Coming into mastery calls for accepting a problem, trying out ways to resolve it, and sticking with the struggle until a conclusion of some sort, tentative though it may be, has been reached. Mastering also calls for minding one's own business. In the final analysis, this is what we mean when we talk about making the world our own through the exercise of natural powers in the pursuit of meaningful purposes.

William Cooper Howells, born in Wales in 1807, was brought to the United States the following year, the family settling eventually in Steubenville, Ohio. Young William's schooling through age ten was confined to three winter terms. But he became a newspaperman— writer, correspondent, editor—and finally a member of the consular service. "Adverse fortune," as his fastidious son, novelist William Dean Howells, saw it, made his father "contented with makeshifts in the material and aesthetic results he aimed at." And so in consequence

... he was not a very good draughtsman, not a very good poet, not a very good editor, according to the several standards of our more settled times; but he was the very best *man* I have ever known.[18]

Like his father, William Dean was mostly self-educated. His aim was higher, his opportunities more numerous; but father and son were both their own men.

Working for mastery sometimes has remained apart from schooling in times closer yet. In the 1890's and early 1900's, Mother Jones, pioneer child advocate and labor organizer, found many working children for whom school held little meaning. She reports a conversation with one ten-year-old tobacco-chewing trapper boy.

[17] Albert Camus. *Notebooks: 1942-1951*. Justin O'Brien, translator. New York: Alfred A. Knopf, Inc., 1965. p. 141. Copyright © by Alfred A. Knopf, Inc.

[18] William Cooper Howells. *Recollections of Life in Ohio from 1813 to 1840*. New York, 1895. Reprint, with an introduction by Edwin H. Cady. Gainesville, Florida: Scholars' Facsimiles and Reprints, 1963. p. v.

"Why don't you go to school?"

"Gee," he said—though it was really something stronger—"I ain't lost no leg."

I knew what he meant: the lads went to school when they were incapacitated by accidents.[19]

Opening and closing doors for mule-drawn coal cars was something to be learned at the mine, not in school.

Simmie Free, a native Georgian born in 1892, is now retired from two lifelong pursuits, hunting and moonshining, at both of which he is held by his neighbors to have been pretty good. "I don't listen to what nobody tells me," he declared recently.

Well, I did one time. When I stayed out a'school t'go a'huntin', the teacher asked me why didn't I come to school. I listened to her. Then I told her I'd rather hunt. I got graduated from the second grade and didn't go no further. And I've hunted all my life ever since.[20]

To his mind mastering did not call for school. Fact of the matter, school seemed to get in the way.

We have laid out a rationale in support of putting the drive for mastering in the middle of an equal rights curriculum for children. All learners take on the world as well as they can and wrest from it whatever satisfaction it has to offer, making sense out of what happens to them as they go. They try first one way and then another to make life yield up what it has to offer. As masterers of their circumstances, they keep at it until something gives—and then deploy their forces for the next onslaught a little farther up the hill. The drive for mastering life has to be understood as residing deep in each child, taking shape as personal powers come into play in pursuit of purposes meaningful to the individual.

Thus, if we are serious about helping children who have been undertaught, overtaught, mistaught, or not taught some things at all, then trying to relate schooling more directly to the drive for mastering would seem to be in order.

[19] Mary Jones. In: Mary F. Parton, editor. *The Autobiography of Mother Jones.* Chicago: Charles H. Kerr Publishing Company, 1974. Copyright © 1925. pp. 130-31. Third edition.

[20] "Simmie Free." In: Eliot Wigginton, editor. *Foxfire 3.* Garden City, New York: Doubleday & Company, Inc., 1975. p. 53. From *The Foxfire Book.* Copyright © 1968, 1969, 1970, 1971, 1972 by The Foxfire Fund, Inc. Reprinted by permission.

A Framework for Change

What do we mean by mastering? What new elements or emphases are called for if we really mean business about helping all children learn what they can learn, have the right to learn, and should learn? What about the natural or personal powers of which we have been talking so optimistically? How far can we depend on these in our effort to re-develop the curriculum for children? Answers here will bring us face to face with the kind of changes that have to come in our thinking before we can get very far.

Mastering as a Mode of Learning

Digging in and doing what they must to make the world their own . . . wresting from the world whatever it has to offer . . . triumphing over circumstances . . . striving . . . pursuing . . . trying . . . minding their own business . . . deploying their forces for the next onslaught a little higher up the hill—these are the ways in which we have talked about master-ing. But we can be more specific.

Focus. A need or problem of some kind has to be recognized and accepted by the learner before the drive for mastery can come into play. Confusion, ambiguity, lack of fit, unassimilability of new experience— all are states in which focus comes into being as lack of present compe-tence makes itself felt. For the infant and young child, every day offers a hundred such instances of need. Older children, especially when they have been grounded in school, may have to be helped to feel needs or define problems. What do I not know? Or better: what do I need to learn? If mastering is to become an active process, focus has to come first.

Even when children have a sturdy base of adventuring to draw on, as we have contended that all children should have, the finding of focus can be time consuming. Perhaps the best approach is to regard focus-finding as a problem in itself. The first characteristic of thinking, as Dewey defines it, is "facing the facts—inquiry, minute and extensive scrutinizing, observation."[21] From "confrontation with the facts" can emerge an awareness of what we can already handle and what we cannot, where we are and where we might want to go.

---

[21] John Dewey. *Reconstruction in Philosophy.* Boston: Beacon Press, 1948; first published 1920. pp. 140-41.

Foresight. Mastering takes time. Once the target has been set or sighted, then getting to it is the issue at hand. Unless children know where they want to go, they can hardly be expected to plot the course. Practice, patience, and pertinacity combine to take the young learner into the clearing.

The remarkable thing about the road to mastering the world is the capacity of learners to keep the end in view. Sometimes it is a matter of growing into it; the goal may lie beyond partly because the learner is not physically able to realize it, even with all the will at his disposal. Sometimes it is the simple fact that skill comes from experience. "Practice makes perfect" is a principle that still makes a lot of sense. Moreover, mastering becomes increasingly demanding as success comes along. The next level of competence lies just ahead and often merges with and supplants the achievement of a goal reached and surpassed almost without a young striver's knowing it.

Action. Focus and foresight set the scene. Then comes the exercise of the learner's powers. Mastering is by definition active. While it may be guided or even directed up to a point, the achievement of mastery calls for the would-be achiever to put forth effort and expend energy. Some skills, it is true, may be usefully introduced in passive or responsive practice sessions. But skills cannot make much difference until they are incorporated into the lives of learners. And that takes doing. Application is the name of the game.

The language we are using may seem on the strenuous side. However, the overly passive schooling of children is very much at issue. The undertaught children of whom we have spoken do not get much from responsive skills teaching alone. Who could care less whether the questions have all been answered or the blanks filled in? Overtaught children—what a waste of time it is for them, too, to be confined to a paper-and-pencil curriculum. All children are mistaught, we might argue, if they get the idea that this is what mastering the world is all about.

Powers cannot be strengthened unless they are fully exercised. Interest can be aroused and maintained only as an increase in personal effectiveness makes itself felt. And skills—any way we wish to define them—become a part of us only as we make them our own. Countless attempts to solve problems that have genuine meaning for us—that seems to be what it takes.

Passive learning will not do. Give-it-back-to-me teaching aims too low; it settles for too little. If we mean business about an equal rights curriculum for children, we have to hope for more.

Proficiency vs. Deficiency: a New Model

Children come to us more alike than different. All of them, from their lifelong exercise of natural powers, are more competent than incompetent in finding satisfaction in their experience, making sense out of it, and choosing wisely among their options. All of them will have uniquenesses in their repertoire. Some will know more songs, some will be more adept at finding a friend, some readier to laugh or cry. Some children will have more questions stored up, some more guesses to try out. Some will want to know why oftener than others, some will be more dogged and deliberate in everything they do. But these are differences that we expect. Our variety and richness as a people make for differences in personal experience.

Standards. Yet in the past, when children have reached us, more often than not we have interpreted differences as deficiencies. And in consequence we have arrayed against children—and against ourselves as professionals—a set of noxious notions even now not entirely forsaken. They ran or run something like this:

Some children can learn, some cannot.

The former come from favored environments, the latter from other kinds of environments.

Success in school can be assured only by adjustment of standards to ability and achievement levels.

Obviously, schooling cannot be expected to compensate, try as we may, for deficiencies that rest on or arise from the very nature of things.

Curriculum provisions, varied to fit what can be expected of different kinds of children, will range from remediation to enrichment.

The idea that all children should be taught what all children need to know is out of the question.

Fortunately, this deficiency model is being replaced very rapidly by what we may call a proficiency model (see Exhibit 9). We have joined forces—the public and our profession—to reject a no-can-do outlook upon the education of all our children. And more than anything else, what this calls for is the revival of standards of achievement.

Exhibit 9. Proficiency Model of Learning vs. Deficiency Model

Proficiency Model	Aspects of Model	Deficiency Model
Natural powers in common	Nature of learners	Range of abilities Differences in interests and talents
Past experience Prior training	Forces bearing on learner	Class Racial-ethnic group Family income Sex Place of residence
Diagnosis Prescription Continuous testing (feedback) Variation in materials	Strategies of teaching	Adjustment of assignments to ability or level of prior achievement Individualization through pacing
Everyone at work Variation in approach	Responses to instruction	Variation in application Acceptance by some, rejection by others Differences in rate of learning
Some common learnings Mastery of specified learnings	Expected outcomes	Differences in level of achievement Progress related to where learner began "Success" an individual matter
Common content covered by all Possible variation in approaches Some content unique to learner	Curriculum provisions	Adjustment in relation to ability or level of prior achievement Enrichment for some, remediation for others

Children come to us competent in the use of their powers but different, too, in the shape and scope of their achievement. Now, if our job is to contribute to the effective functioning of all children, we must decide what every child needs to function effectively and then make sure that he already has what he needs or gets it in school. This means valuing proficiency and setting goals for its attainment. Thus we return to the matter of mastering.

True mastery. The revival of standards of mastery is already well under way. The pioneer in the contemporary movement to revivify specificity in the framing of learning objectives has followed through with inescapable logic. According to Benjamin Bloom, 95 percent of all students should be able to learn facts and skills of the kind that can be set forth to be mastered. What it takes is dealing intelligently with differences in pace, energy, learning style, knowledge, and aptitude. A variety of methods, materials, and systems of peer-adult support must be available. Continuous assessment—diagnosis, monitoring, and final evaluation—has to be integral to the process. And of course staff curriculum planning and self-supervision must be in the picture.[22]

Can we accept and act on this new optimism? Half our mind says we must, half our mind—for some of us—may say we can't. Many persons are trying to marry the old and the new. Specify objectives, individualize instruction, work for step-by-step mastery—yes. No child will ever again fail to learn, all will succeed in moving ahead. However, when we take a closer look at most of the programs built on these premises, ahead of the game though they may be in many ways, we still find children strung out as usual along a continuum from little learning to much. This kind of halfway effort begs the question. Mastery that is not defined in terms of achievement standards set for all children is not true mastery.

No doubt it will take us a while yet to get our thoughts in order. But we are on our way. A proficiency model based on an understanding of natural powers and a grasp of and respect for the extent of children's competence, and that accepts our professional responsibility to get results with every child, will prevail as it must.

The Powers at Our Command

Nature sends children into the world with great gifts at their command. From the beginning, infants reach out to gain satisfaction from their surroundings. They soon devote most of their waking moments to making increasing sense out of the world. As choices identify themselves, children become ever better able to act to make the most of their experience. Nature's gifts or powers, as we are calling them, are at our command from the word go. Their exercise and strengthening ensures survival, growth, development. As we seek occasions for the exercise of our natural powers toward becoming more competent and thus more in command, we recognize that life itself is

---

[22] Benjamin Bloom. "Mastery Learning and Its Implications." In: Elliot W. Eisner, editor. *Confronting Curriculum Reform*. Boston: Little, Brown and Company, 1971. pp. 17-49.

the grand curriculum. But, organized as a vital part of life experience, schooling has a unique role to play.

Practice. Competence and command develop whether schooling is there or not. After all, formal schooling for children is a newcomer on the stage of world history. But schooling when it is successful can make a great difference. One of its major functions, as we have noted, is to specify facts and skills that contribute to mastering the world and to make sure that these are learned.

Incorporation of new learnings that will strengthen the competence of children can begin, as it often does, with brief practice sessions. Here is something we think you will find useful if you do not already have it in hand. Try it out. Work on it a bit. How did it go? Work on it a little more. Economy indicates the wisdom of using group instruction or self-study procedures or some combination of the two for initial skills practice.

Application. However, such practice is not an end in itself. All of us agree that mastery can come to children only through repeated use of new learnings in the pursuit and realization of meaningful purposes. Children have to see the difference it makes when they tackle a problem with a new way of working. Then, through many applications, they find themselves moving onto a new level of competence. The exercise of their powers as strengthened is more satisfying, more sense making, yields new options all the way around.

Our concern in teaching the facts and skills that attend or implement mastery has always been that of balancing out practice and application. If we can hold in mind the necessity of keeping the exercise of children's natural powers in focus and devoting the proper amount of time to foresight and action, then we may be able to do better than we have with teaching all children what they need to know in order to function effectively. (See Exhibit 10 for a simple attempt to relate the exercise of natural powers to representative learning activities.)

Command. The powers at our command: what does this mean? We are born to make the world our own. Living and learning combine to develop our powers to do so. At any point along the way, we have command over our circumstances to the extent that our powers are adequate to the demands made upon them. In due time, we may suppose, if our experience remains rich and varied and our education relevant to our needs and if our energy holds out, we will come into full command

Exhibit 10. Natural Powers and Their Exercise:
Sample Learning Activities

Natural Powers	Sample Activities
1. *Performing* acting acting out gaming interpreting operating playing practicing putting on role playing taking part in	Choosing a poem and reading it aloud Playing a new tag game Putting on a puppet show based on a familiar story Singing a song that no one else knows Climbing a rope
2. *Bonding* befriending communing contending dialoguing interacting joining loving relating sharing working together	Welcoming a newcomer to the class Planning a trip to the art museum Sharing the results of a field study of native grasses Pairing off for practice of number facts Discussing an event in the news
3. *Expressing* feeling giving out going out to grieving reacting rejoicing reporting responding to revealing voicing	Retelling a favorite tale Moving to music Talking about what makes us happy or sad Making a list of famous persons we would like to know Telling about something funny that happened to a friend
4. *Finding out* discovering experimenting inquiring investigating measuring problem-solving questioning searching seeking testing	Determining area needed for garden plot Looking up information about canal boat days Interviewing adults on how they feel about space exploration Testing strength of various adhesives Finding out about different kinds of birds' nests

Natural Powers	Sample Activities
5. *Making* classifying composing constructing generalizing inventing organizing planning putting together shaping theorizing	Mapping school neighborhood in terms of types of housing Composing music for Halloween Writing a report, "What We Have Learned about Bees" Making a clay animal Designing a school for the future
6. *Controlling* changing contending directing managing persuading preparing projecting teaching trying out willing	Tutoring a classmate in something she/he missed while out sick Being in charge of cleanup crew for week Running for class or school office Preparing arguments for change in school regulations Proposing new room layout to be tried
7. *Valuing* affirming appraising celebrating choosing exalting honoring judging questing for reflecting on worshiping	Setting up options for open time each week Reading biographies of persons who have helped mankind Determining criteria for selection of citizen of the week Discussing problem stories read aloud Keeping track of own use of weekend time
8. *Persisting* coming back to enduring hanging onto holding on resisting resolving returning to reviving surviving trying	Taking skills test, noting needs, keeping progress record Planning time schedule for an independent study project Keeping journal of thoughts and ideas Checking file of written work periodically Using study periods to work on specified goals

of our powers. We will have come through. To the extent that this is possible, we will be able to make the world our own.

For children, of course, we settle for along-the-way mastery and control. To the extent that children learn what they can use to meet their needs and realize their purposes, they may be said to be in command of their purposes. Competence is always relative, we may decide.

Command comes into force—and this is our message here—as new learning proves enabling. Practice may serve to introduce useful facts and skills, application to integrate and consolidate them in children's behavior. The true test of mastery, however, is found in a genuine increase in personal effectiveness. Does the learning make a difference in the world beyond the school?

Schooling has to be put to this ultimate test. Doing well in school is where we start. How can the drive for mastery best be sustained? What matters most in the exercise and strengthening of personal powers? We have tried to address ourselves to these questions.

But doing well in the wider world—we also have to keep our eye on that. Some things are surely more worth learning than others if we are concerned about ensuring full development to all children. Thus, we return to the basic curriculum question: What facts and skills most need to be mastered?

Extensions of Content: Some Possibilities

Adventuring provides a hard-to-beat base for learning of many kinds and degrees. Exploring the natural and built environments and the cultural realm, child adventurers have some worthwhile experiences that hardly call for formalization in terms of levels or standards of learning. The sensuous impact of sky and woods and water, the surprise of coming upon hidden-away aspects of town or city, the delight of first-time encounters with memorable music or art or drama—these are good in themselves. Adventurers also gain valuable learnings related to the scope and use of our various environments, from which they may begin to develop and test out guidelines for providing a total environment that will be better for us all. And, of course, as we have noted, experience in the broader world yields impressions, images, and information relevant to learnings in many subject fields.

Mastering is a way of learning that aims at bringing a piece of the world of experience under control. Through focus, foresight, and action, the young learner strives to attain standards of competence that will ensure true mastery. Specified facts and skills are practiced and then applied in many problem-solving situations through which the powers of the learner are brought more fully into command.

In which fields, we are now ready to ask, do facts and skills most need to be mastered as we work to develop an equal rights curriculum for children? Here are our proposals for possible extensions of content.

Mastering the Fundamentals

We include the mastering of fundamentals among extensions of content for two reasons. First, we are pledged to the successful teaching of the basics to all children—and that is certainly new! Second, we propose that the fundamentals as usually defined be somewhat broadened.

Reading. The teaching of reading seems to be poised on the brink of a breakthrough. Hope of finding the one and only way to do it has given ground to faith in a vigorous eclecticism.[23] "Let's make use of everything that works" seems to be the new principle of operation, well illustrated by the imaginative Right To Read attempt to locate and validate programs that get unexpected results. The reconciliation of the experience approach with direct teaching of sound-symbol relationships, the provision of ingeniously conceived manipulative and self-study materials, the refinement of diagnostic devices, the flooding of classrooms with high quality paperbacks, the growth of school libraries or materials centers—all are signs of forces at work that promise to go much beyond our previous success in teaching all children to read.

We have assurance, too, that what we are trying to do will really pay off. Much has been learned from linguistics about the nature of language, the acquisition of language by children, the impact of dialectal differences on reading, problems of bilingualism, the act of reading itself. New rigor has gone into identification of objectives and preparation of materials. Interest is back in the picture as a factor of reading and so is the place of literature—but perhaps these are one and the same thing. And the psychological underpinnings of individualized reading instruction are more widely understood.

"Why don't you teach our children to read?" Before long we may

---

[23] Guy L. Bond and Robert Dykstra. "The Cooperative Research Program in First-Grade Reading Instruction." *Reading Research Quarterly* 2: 1-142; Summer 1967; also, John B. Carroll and Jeanne Chall, editors. *Towards a Literate Society.* The Report of the Committee on Reading, National Academy of Education. New York: McGraw-Hill Book Company, 1975.

not ever again have to listen to this heart-wrung and heartbreaking question. Meantime, we must keep our pressure up.

Language development. Spelling, as Edward Eggleston reported in *The Hoosier Schoolmaster* (1871), was "the one branch diligently taught in a backwoods school" in mid-nineteenth century America.

> It often happens that the pupil does not know the meaning of a single word in the lesson. This is of no consequence. What do you want to know the meaning of a word for? Words were made to be spelled, and men were probably created that they might spe'l them. Hence the necessity for sending a pupil through the spelling-book five times before you allow him to begin to read, or indeed to do anything else. Hence the necessity for those long spelling-classes at the close of each forenoon and afternoon session of the school, to stand at the head of which is the cherished ambition of every scholar. Hence, too, the necessity for devoting the whole of the afternoon session of each Friday to a "spelling-match." [24]

Spelling has long since been subordinated to reading and related more closely to composition. Handwriting, another prestigious skill of the era, has been redefined as one of the lesser arts. About all that is left out front among the old-time school-stressed language skills is grammar and usage. Despite the interest engendered in the new grammar during the late 1960's, no one seems quite sure what part the formal study of language should play in the education of children. We can predict that its status, however, will not rise much unless or until it can be related to growth in power to use language.

The fact is that the scope and focus of language arts is up for grabs. The most promising prospect is that composition, both oral and written, may become the integrating principle of the new language arts. Never really out front as it might have been, the importance of composition has new support from a number of sources. Many approaches to beginning reading use the learner's own sentences and stories. Our interest in independent study in its several guises gives us new respect for the function of composition in the various subject fields. Perhaps our new appreciation of dialect also contributes to our concern for effectiveness in the use of oral and written language.

Most compelling from our point of view is that language development is integral to or coincident with the exercise and strengthening of almost every one of the natural powers: expressing, interacting, finding out, making, and so on. Competence in this area undergirds performance

[24] Chapter 2, "A Spell Coming."

everywhere. Thus, mastering the use of language in speaking and writing becomes of great importance in an equal rights curriculum.

Mathematics and science. "Strengthen the female mind by enlarging it, and there will be an end of blind obedience"—this was Mary Wollstonecraft's outcry against the impoverished education of women in *A Vindication of the Rights of Woman* (1792). The Seneca Falls convention on women's rights, in its historic *Declaration of Sentiments* (1848), included educational disenfranchisement among man's wrongs: "He has denied her the facilities for obtaining a thorough education, all colleges being closed against her." And as for vocations:

> He has monopolized nearly all the profitable employments, and from those she is permitted to follow, she receives but a scanty remuneration. He closes against her all the avenues to wealth and distinction which he considers most honorable to himself. As a teacher of theology, medicine, or law, she is not known.[25]

A few years earlier, in her *Woman in the Nineteenth Century* (1845), Margaret Fuller had staked out the vocational claims of women in these stirring words: "Let them be sea-captains, if you will."[26] In our times, concern for the educational-vocational constriction experienced by girl or woman is expressed in more direct terms:

> As she goes through school she learns that subjects which teach mastery and control over the world, such as science and math, are male subjects; while subjects which teach appearance, maintenance, or sentiment, such as home economics or literature, are female subjects. School counselors will recommend nursing for girls, while they will encourage boys to be doctors.[27]

Let us put mathematics and science together as the hard subjects to which it was thought historically only boys of well-to-do families needed to have access. Actually, school proficiency in the "hard" subjects may still be related to some extent to class and income as well as gender and perhaps to place of residence and racial-ethnic group membership. Certainly failure to master mathematics in the pre-college years can become a barrier to entry into many of the fields of work to which access is now being more widely sought.

---

[25] For an account of the convention and its background, see: Miriam Gurko. *The Ladies of Seneca Falls: The Birth of the Woman's Rights Movement.* New York: Macmillan Publishing Co., Inc., 1974.

[26] Quoted in Gurko, *op. cit.,* p. 78.

[27] "Politics of the Ego: A Manifesto for New York Radical Feminists (1969)." In: Judith Hole and Ellen Levine. *Rebirth of Feminism.* New York: Quadrangle Books, 1971. p. 445.

Content in both elementary school mathematics and science seems to be resettling after the effort of academicians to "modernize" it during the 60's. The return to respect for operations in mathematics and the apparent edge of process over structure in science would seem to promise a renewed concern for mastery of the fundamentals in these fields. At least, this seems likely in mathematics; sad to say, competence in science has never been of much interest in the education of children.

We are contending that nothing will do more to equalize the curriculum than a straightforward, all-out effort to bring both mathematics and science into the arena of subjects to be thoroughly liked and thoroughly learned by all children.

Getting a Hold on the Constructive Arts

Mastering the fundamentals in the academic areas may be where we start. But if we intend to help children make the world their own, we must extend our concern to include mastering in other areas. One of these is what we may call the constructive arts. William James has described, as well as anyone, the basis of our long-established interest in this field:

> Up to the eighth or ninth year of childhood one may say that the child does hardly anything else than handle objects, explore things with his hands, doing and undoing, setting up and knocking down, putting together and pulling apart; for, from the psychological point of view, construction and destruction are two names for the same manual activity. Both signify the production of change, and the working of effects, in outward things. The result of all this is that intimate familiarity with the physical environment, that acquaintance with the properties of material things, which is really the foundation of human consciousness.[28]

Guidance and direction of such exploration in the school setting can and should lead to greater competence than could be obtained by children working entirely on their own.

Practical and home arts. Renewed respect is being expressed for the role of industrial arts and home economics as we work to revivify the function of interest and activity in the education of children. Dewey, who did so much to alert teachers to the value of "active occupations," warned against the impulse to provide formed rather than raw materials and to pre-teach the use of tools and materials, "assuming that pupils

[28] William James. *Talks to Teachers.* New York: Henry Holt and Company, 1916. pp. 58-59.

cannot learn how [to use them] in the process of making." Children learn most and best through "the course of intelligent (that is, purposeful) use of things." For example, how different is the

> . . . attitude of a boy in making, say, a kite, with respect to the grain and other properties of wood, the matter of size, angles, and proportion of parts, to the attitude of a pupil who has an object-lesson on a piece of wood, where the sole function of wood and its properties is to serve as subject matter for the lesson.[29]

These same admonitions will no doubt be worth keeping in mind as we try to provide children with more opportunities to develop skill in using saws and scissors and measuring cups to deal with wood, cloth, and foodstuffs.

We will probably also want to enlarge our expectations of what can come from manipulative activity. Henri Bergson spoke of the proneness to regard work with the hands as relaxation only.

> We forget that the intellect is essentially the faculty of manipulating matter, that it at least began by being so, that such was nature's intention. Why then should the intellect not profit by manual training? We can go further and say that it is quite natural for the child to try its hand at constructing. By helping it, by furnishing it at least with opportunities, one would later obtain from the grown man a superior yield; one would greatly increase what inventiveness there is in the world.[30]

Or so we hope.

Arts and crafts. Ahead of us, poet and novelist Robert Penn Warren predicts, may lie real leisure, a product of the dreaded technology, in which many of us may be free to practice the arts. Rescue from impersonalization may come through "the made thing" or personal creation by which an individual can express "an affirmation of his sense of life."[31]

The arts and crafts have long been valued in childhood education. Time for mastering the processes involved in shaping clay, weaving, basket making, and the like may sometimes have been scanted. But our renewal of interest in both activity learning and the arts may give us

---

[29] John Dewey. *Democracy and Education.* New York: Macmillan Publishing Co., Inc., 1916. p. 233.

[30] Henri Bergson. *The Creative Mind.* M. L. Anderson, translator. New York: Philosophical Library, 1946. p. 100.

[31] Robert Penn Warren. *Democracy and Poetry.* Cambridge, Massachusetts: Harvard University Press, 1975. p. 89.

reason to reserve more time for an area where all too often in the past the most highly advantaged children have been the only ones likely to receive really first-rate instruction.

Project work. Constructive activities that cut across several fields of work are familiar to all of us. Their values became evident in the latter decades of the nineteenth century as the work of the great German educator Tuiskon Ziller (1817-1883) became known in this country. Coordination, articulation, or concentration of studies around selected themes was the essence of his proposals. Typical American adaptations included such project activities as these for a third-grade study based on the reading of *Robinson Crusoe:*

1. Picturing of Robinson, showing his field of grain, his harvest

2. Drawing a stalk of wheat, a sheaf of wheat: a saber used as a scythe; pestle and mortar used in pounding wheat; etc.

3. Molding of saber, pestle, mortar, basket, plate, and loaf

4. Paper-cutting: saber, basket, mortar, pestle.[32]

Of course, all this was accompanied by related activities in science, music, mathematics, and written language.

Closer to home is the rich literature on the project method published in the United States between 1910 and 1935. A textbook by Alice M. Krackowizer[33] may stand as a prime example. She presents purposeful activities of many kinds, with photographs of children at work as well as projects completed in primary methods classes. One chapter classifies constructive activities as growing out of play (play house, cart, airplane), the social motive (gifts, refreshments), gardening and farm visits (seed labels, butter making), and drama (accessories, artifacts for historical plays).

Project work has received renewed attention in our own times as classrooms (and shared teaching spaces) have been reorganized to foster independent study, with due attention to activities that may draw upon learnings in more than one subject field.

Altogether various kinds of constructive arts have long been considered important in the education of children and are now newly valued.

[32] Charles De Garmo. *Herbart and the Herbartians.* New York: Charles Scribner's Sons, 1896. pp. 126-27.

[33] Alice M. Krackowizer. *Projects in the Primary Grades.* Philadelphia: J. B. Lippincott Company, 1919.

Mastering what it takes to perform well in these areas needs to be included in any equal rights curriculum.

Managing the Body

When Black Elk (born in 1860) was five years old, grandfather gave him his first bow and arrows, and he and his playfellows began to wage war. Running in naked bands, they warded off enemies with mud balls and willow sticks. By the age of nine

> I was growing taller and was riding horses now and could shoot prairie chickens and rabbits with my bow. The boys of my people began very young to learn the ways of men, and no one taught us; we just learned by doing what we saw . . .[34]

Sioux boys grew up in command of their bodies.

In East Lansing, Michigan, after their father's death, Malcolm X and his brothers became hunters and providers, selling rabbits to neighbors and foraging for other creatures of value.

> We would trap muskrats out in the little creek in back of our house. And we would lie quiet until unsuspecting bullfrogs appeared, and we would spear them, cut off their legs, and sell them for a nickel a pair to people who lived up and down the road.[35]

Competence in managing bodies—and lives, too—comes early for some children.

Sissy Jupe, girl number twenty at Gradgrind's school in Charles Dickens' *Hard Times* (1854), was such another. While she could not define a horse to the master's satisfaction (the odious Bitzer could: "Quadruped. Graminivorous. Forty teeth," etc.), she had grown up in a traveling horse show in which her father was a comic acrobat. And Sissy could tumble well enough to be a part of his act. In what counted for most, she was competent—although her poor father wanted more for her, so much more.

Managing the body is of first concern to all children. Helping them gain ever greater competence ought to be of comparable importance to the school. Children who come to us with a high level of physical

[34] John G. Neihardt. *Black Elk Speaks: Being the Life Story of a Holy Man of the Ogalala Sioux.* New York: Pocket Books, a division of Simon & Schuster, Inc., 1972. p. 17. Courtesy of the John G. Neihardt Trust, Hilda Neihardt Petri, Trustee.

[35] Malcolm X with the assistance of Alex Haley. *The Autobiography of Malcolm X.* New York: Grove Press, Inc., 1965. p. 14. Copyright © 1964 by Alex Haley and Malcolm X. Copyright © 1965 by Alex Haley and Betty Shabazz. Reprinted by permission of Grove Press, Inc.

effectiveness may find little awareness or appreciation of what they are able to do and little assistance in moving ahead. For those who have much to learn, continued inequality may affect success in other aspects of development as well.

Play. Free play is the base for growth of body management outside of school and may well remain so inside, particularly for younger children. Do we sometimes fear that playtime may be a waste of teaching time? Let us concede that children at play must be their own teachers. If we need to keep busy, perhaps we can take a closer look at play conditions. The adventure playground and play park movement, in which interaction with raw or throwaway materials is largely substituted for performance on fixed equipment, deserves far more attention than we have given it.[36] Moreover, if we hope for free play to develop into creative enterprises, we may need to think again about the allotment of time as a constricting condition.

Directed movement. "Movement is one of man's languages and as such it must be consciously mastered." So Rudolf Laban (1879-1958) contended.[37] This leader of movement education invented a set of concepts still under study by physical educators. But his definition of movement as "living architecture" can be appreciated by all of us as well as his reference to "biological innocents." Proficiency in movement or body management or use of motor skills, wherever we prefer to start, is learned and thus can be taught. Walking, running, and jumping . . . lifting and carrying . . . bending and balancing . . . crawling and climbing . . . throwing and catching . . . rising and growing, sinking and shrinking . . . stalking the prey, circling in tribute to the hunters . . . moving to music as dance—the targets proposed for mastery of movement are many and varied. But conscious learning and directed teaching are both to be in the picture. Free play alone, we are agreed, is not enough.

Organized activities. Is it time for us to reconsider our outlook on games and sports? The attack on Little League sexism may cause us to wonder about school practice. Do we exclude girls from such team sports as we do offer? Do we, in fact, exclude most children by not offering much, fearful as we have been of exploitation and competition?

[36] See: Lady Allen of Hurtwood. *Planning for Play.* Cambridge, Massachusetts: M.I.T. Press, 1969; and Arvid Bengtsson. *Adventure Playgrounds.* New York: Praeger Publishers, 1972.

[37] Rudolf Laban. *The Language of Movement.* Boston: Plays, Inc., 1974. p. viii.

As for singles sports—swimming, tennis, ice skating, running and other field events, and so on—have we given over our responsibility to private clubs and coaches for good reason? Are there, in short, more kinds of modified team activities that we could safely sponsor, more kinds of simplified individual sports? If so, under what conditions?

We may decide to continue as we are. But if we do, we should realize that we are missing out on an opportunity to equalize one kind of learning between the sexes, between children who can afford private lessons and those who cannot, between those who can pick up their interest in a variety of organized activities out of the air, so to speak, and those who must depend on the school to introduce them to such sports and start them off on needed skills.

In the realm of managing the body, mastering can be thought of in terms of play, directed movement, and organized activities. We propose that an equal rights curriculum will put more emphasis on all of these. Everyone has a body to be managed and schooling can help if it will.

Controlling the Self

If one value or virtue were to be named as obsessively American, it would no doubt be self-reliance. "Explore, and explore, and explore," Emerson urged upon the youth of his day. "Be neither chided nor flattered out of your position of perpetual inquiry." [38] Trust in inquiry is at the heart of our commitment. "I like the scientific spirit," old Walt affirmed:

> . . . the holding off, the being sure but not too sure, the willingness to surrender ideas when the evidence is against them . . . it always keeps the way beyond open—always gives life, thought, affection, the whole man, a chance to try over again after a mistake—after a wrong guess. (May 4, 1888) [39]

The narrator in *The Great Gatsby*, having observed the collapse of one misinterpreter of the dream, can still celebrate, even if ironically, the "transitory enchanted moment" when Dutch sailors first caught sight of Long Island Sound. Then

---

[38] "Literary Ethics" (1838). Found in: R. W. Emerson. *Nature, Addresses, and Lectures.* Cambridge, Massachusetts: Harvard University Press, 1971. p. 115.

[39] *Walt Whitman's Camden Conversations.* Selected, arranged, and with an introduction by Walter Teller. New Brunswick, New Jersey: Rutgers University Press, 1973. pp. 168-69.

... man must have held his breath in the presence of this continent, compelled into an aesthetic contemplation he neither understood nor desired, face to face for the last time in history with something commensurate to his capacity for wonder.[40]

As a contemporary spokesman for the vision, Warren takes it for granted that "the self is never to be found, but must be created . . . the product of a thousand actions, large and small." [41]

Most of us would agree that self plays a vital role in learning. We may talk of self-concept or image rather than self-reliance or creation. But trying to free children from a limiting sense of self is one of the remedies for lowered school achievement to which all of us subscribe. Can we add controlling self to the list of realms for mastery that we believe should be highlighted in an equal rights curriculum? Today we have many new ideas to draw on, most of which have been developed outside of the school in the reeducation of adults.

Consciousness. Self-awareness is the first step in moving toward control. How did I get this way? Why am I content? Who did this to me? In pioneer labor politics, the organizer's hardest job was always to jar miners and mill workers out of their torpor. During her later years, Mother Jones was still at it, urging the suffragists to stand for "free speech in the streets" as well as women's rights. How can we when we don't have the vote? Her reply was to be expected:

"I never had a vote," said I, "and I have raised hell all over this country. You don't need a vote to raise hell! You need convictions and a voice!" [42]

When the black hero of the classic *Invisible Man* finally rebelled at trying "to go in everyone's direction but my own," he found his world had become "one of infinite possibilities." [43] Consciousness raising by today's feminists has focused very directly on alerting women to "new models of behavior for men and women." [44]

Choice. Bringing into view new possibilities and models is the first step of working for control of self. Opportunities to make choices that

[40] F. Scott Fitzgerald. *The Great Gatsby.* New York: Charles Scribner's Sons, 1925. p. 182.

[41] Robert Penn Warren, *op. cit.,* p. 89.

[42] Mary Jones, *op. cit.,* p. 203.

[43] Ralph Ellison. *Invisible Man.* New York: Random House, Inc., 1952. pp. 433-35. Copyright © 1952 by Random House, Inc.

[44] M. Kay Martin and Barbara Voorhies, *op. cit.,* p. 409.

will test out options must then be provided. In our definition of mastering as a mode of learning, we have called for focus, foresight, and action. Practice and application are to bring new facts and skills under command. If a more adequate sense of personhood comes "as the product of a thousand actions, large and small," then we believe we are proposing, in our new curriculum, the optimal setting for conscious self-development.

Summary and Conclusion

Have we made our case for reviving and reinstating mastering as a way of learning in an equal rights curriculum for children?

Mastering the fundamentals, getting a hold on the constructive arts, managing the body, and controlling the self: these are areas in which we propose that a new model of proficiency be established. These are the areas, we would contend, in which inequality among children today is most damaging and also perhaps in which a general level of insufficiency could be substantiated.

We contend, in our proposal, that promotion of a process of problem-solving that attends to focus, foresight, and action will yield the desired proficiency in consonance with our commitment to purposeful learning.

We call for the setting up of standards of proficiency to be reached by all children in those aspects of our curriculum that need to be mastered by all.

We argue that teaching for mastery in the past has missed the boat because it did not go far enough to affect and strengthen the exercise of natural powers.

We propose that useful facts and skills, while they may be introduced in practice sessions, can be perfected only through application in pursuits meaningful to the learner.

We are convinced that growth in the powers of the learner—in expressing, finding out, relating, creating, and so on—is the only measure of true mastery.

Adventuring in the natural, built, and cultural environments provides children with many experiences good in themselves, many learnings unique to the given environment, a good general base for learning in the various subject fields. No doubt the same can be said for mastering the facts and skills of the areas we have identified in this chapter: the fundamentals, the constructive arts, physical education, self-understanding. Our goal is the removal of inequality among children who have been undertaught, overtaught, mistaught, or not taught some things at all. We have still more to propose toward that end.

Associating

Reaching out to others: of all the drives that animate us as human beings, this is surely the most powerful. Watching and waiting are never enough. Touching is what it takes. The infant is picked up and held close. The young child, new to a group, spends the first morning mostly on somebody's lap or very close at hand. Two eight-year-olds sit together, turning the pages of the same book, reading and talking about what they read. Can we make better use of this fact of life as we work with all children to help more of them learn the things they need to learn?

What They Do When They Can

People have to get together for all kinds of reasons. Reproduction of ourselves, nurturance of the dependent young—this is where we begin. But most of the reasons for getting together have to do with a world we make, or have made, for ourselves: meanings agreed upon, codes and contracts drawn up, work goals set in common, team ventures of many kinds. Community is the spirit of this world; society is its name. In the larger sense, we are talking about civilization.

Children first seek satisfaction from mother or nurse. Their earliest efforts at sense-making are checked out with whoever is there, older children as well as adults. Framing alternatives and testing them out are processes that almost always involve interaction with others. In short, children learn from a system that exists to sustain and socialize them at the same time.

Nature has equipped children to make the world of social and cultural relationships and agreements their own. If the young are to become functioning members of a society and contributors to its culture, they must exercise and strengthen the power of associating (see Exhibit 11 for a vocabulary that suggests its aims and dimensions). And children do their best, whether there is schooling to help them or not. Much of what they must learn comes from informal sources. But the school can help if it will. And probably in this day, with the claims of cultural pluralism so plainly before us, the charge upon the school to help all children come into their own as members of the larger society has never been more deeply felt.

Can the drive to associate remain vital in school as well as out? What conditions best support the exercise of the power of associating? These are questions that have long concerned us as believers in the education of the whole child and also as members of a free society. What new understandings may prove of greatest use to children in this area?

"The demand is for social intelligence, social power, and social interests," John Dewey was saying a good while ago. "Our resources are (a) the life of the school as a social institution in itself; (b) methods of learning and of doing work; and (c) the school studies or curricu-

Exhibit 11. A Vocabulary of Associating: Aims and Dimensions

accepting	confronting	interacting	relating
agreeing	contending	joining	settling
aiding	contracting	leading	sharing
arguing	contradicting	linking	soothing
assisting	contributing	loving	supporting
attracting	cooperating	meeting	taking
befriending	debating	opposing	teaming
bonding	deliberating	pacifying	touching
caring for	discussing	pairing	trusting
combining	encountering	participating	uniting
commending	following	partnering	winning
communicating	getting together	pleasing	working together
competing	giving	pooling	
compromising	helping	reconciling	

lum."[1] We would add today another resource—the drive within that comes out in so many dependable ways. Let us reexamine some of these.

Finding Someone To Be With

Some children grow up sustained by relationships within the family. In the old days isolation and poverty could bear hard upon a large farm family. But, as the narrator of one of Joyce Cary's stories recalls it, "We had each other and lived in that wealth of community, of instant comprehension and response, which belongs only to children in a closely knit family."[2] Most children seek other associates, too. The five-year-old who rebelled against enrollment in a public school kindergarten wanted to go to Ethel's school instead. But that is a Catholic school, his mother pointed out.

I raced upstairs to give Ethel the bad news. She took it well yet seemed bemused.

"If you're not Catholic, what are you?" she wondered.

"I'll go downstairs and find out," I offered, wondering what was left.[3]

School can separate friends. But new friends are to be found in any kindergarten.

And in the neighborhood as well. There was another Ethel, who had died of spinal meningitis. When Mrs. Kiest is baking, Ethel's friend next door sniffs the air and decides to pay a call.

"Would you like some coffee cake?" Mrs. Kiest asks, and he always remembers to say thank you as she hands him a sizeable piece, still warm from the oven. Mrs. Kiest and the little boy have something that binds them together besides his love of eating and her pleasure in watching him do it. He and Ethel Kiest did not always play amicably, but when they quarreled he could get up and go home, safe in the knowledge that the next time he saw her it would be forgotten, and now he misses her. He remembers her very clearly and so does Mrs. Kiest.[4]

Memories can build bonds of friendship. Some friends can be grown up. Eating together is one way to get together. How much there is to learn about finding someone to be with . . . and how important it all is.

[1] John Dewey. "Ethical Principles Underlying Education." In: *The Third Yearbook of the National Herbart Society*. Chicago: University of Chicago Press, 1897. p. 26.

[2] Joyce Cary. *Except the Lord*. New York: Harper & Row, Publishers, 1953. p. 4.

[3] Nelson Algren. "Previous Days." In: *The Last Carousel*. New York: G. P. Putnam's Sons, 1973. p. 213. Copyright © 1973 by Nelson Algren. Reprinted by permission of G. P. Putnam's Sons.

[4] William Maxwell. *Ancestors*. New York: Alfred A. Knopf, Inc., 1971. p. 276.

Associating occupies so much of life that we might expect more attention would be paid to how to get started on it. Even for the youngest children, the chief certainty we have gained from a century or more of expressed concern for their social development is to provide setups that call for cooperative work and play—big blocks, a playhouse, and so on. And after the earliest years, we have tended to think of social interaction as likely to impede rather than advance the learning we value most. Study time has been quiet time.

Some of today's approaches to individualized instruction may allow a little more room for associating. But most of them also maximize—and boast about it—the chance of being on your own and doing your own work. What a denial this all seems to be of the life drive to learn how to relate to others. Don't we care about opening up for children in every way we can easier and fuller access to that part of the world that has been made by people working together and which must be maintained by social enterprise? Of course we do. And new help for us as well as for children is quietly coming into existence all around us.

Comparing Notes

In making sense out of the social end of things, children compare notes just as they do when they are confirming and correcting new concepts in the intellectual realm. They also test their insights in action, in this case, in the context of other people. Sometimes the arena for testing is provided by people at home. The youngest of several brothers wonders about the family's welcome for a newborn first sister.

"What ya going to do Papa? Put her in a gunnysack and throw her into Whiskey Creek?" [5]

That's what they did with unwanted kittens. Such childish misperceptions become part of the folklore of every family.

Sometimes the context is larger. Langston Hughes describes a revival at his Auntie Reed's church. He and a friend, both 12, remained unsaved. The rest had gone forward. "Won't you come to Jesus?" It was hot and grew late.

Finally Westley said to me in a whisper: "God damn! I'm tired o' sitting here. Let's go up and be saved." So he got up and was saved.[6]

[5] Jesse W. Hofer. *An Amish Boy Remembers.* San Antonio, Texas: Naylor Company, 1973. p. 119.
[6] Langston Hughes. *The Big Sea: An Autobiography.* New York: Hill and Wang, 1966; first published 1940. p. 19. Reprinted by permission of Farrar, Straus & Giroux, Inc.

But young Langston was still trying to "see Jesus." At last he, too, stood up and was led to the platform. That night he cried when he went to bed. His aunt woke up and told his uncle the boy was crying because he had been saved.

But I was really crying because I couldn't bear to tell her that I had lied, that I had deceived everybody in the church, that I hadn't seen Jesus, and that now I didn't believe there was a Jesus any more, since he didn't come to help me.[7]

The impact of testing a new way of behaving can be private and painful.

Everyone who grows up socially sensitive and adept at relating to others has learned from many chances to check out insights and ideas and put them to the test in social situations. Competence will be defined somewhat differently from one subculture to another, from one age group to another. The school has a vital role to play in offering all children new contacts, new arenas for social learning—as well as guided or directed study and application of useful social understandings and skills.

Holding Their Own

From Staten Island, in October of 1843, Thoreau reported home on the 20 or more trips he had thus far made across the peaceful water to the crush and crowds of Manhattan Island. "It must have a very bad influence on children," he wrote, "to see so many human beings at once —mere herds of men."[8] Looking about him during World War II, the Roumanian playwright, Eugene Ionesco, wondered about the survival of intelligence in man. "Perhaps bees and ants were once intelligent," intelligence being only a "transitory form of adaptation." Could it be that humanity "is evolving toward an ant civilization, a sound and stable organization without revolution and without feeling"?[9] Reflecting on schooling today, as compared with his own as he recalls it, novelist Stuart Cloete (b. 1897) is distressed. "Education has become a method of training the young to fit into a slot in the industrial or com-

[7] *Ibid.*, p. 21.

[8] Walter Harding and Carl Bode, editors. *The Correspondence of Henry David Thoreau.* New York: New York University, 1958. p. 142. Copyright © 1968 by New York University Press. Reprinted by permission.

[9] Eugene Ionesco. *Present Past, Past Present: A Personal Memoir.* Helen R. Lane, translator. New York: Grove Press, Inc., 1971. p. 135. Copyright © 1971 by Grove Press, Inc. Reprinted by permission.

mercial machine rather than a means of developing an independent intellect."[10]

To some degree, associating brings every child under threat. The herd, the ant civilization, the machine—will it take over? Elizabeth Gurley Flynn, spokeswoman of radical politics in the first half of this century, may have had less of a problem. Hers was a politically aware working-class family. "Ideas were our meat and drink, sometimes a substitute for both."[11] Moreover, in the upper grades of P. S. No. 9, she found a debating society that tackled everything from capital punishment to government ownership of trusts. By age 15 she had read or was reading Edward Bellamy's *Looking Backward,* Upton Sinclair's *The Jungle,* Peter Kropotkin's *Appeal to the Young.*

Most children, however, are pretty much on their own in deciding what to accept, what to reject. But they learn fast when they have many others with whom to interact, many opportunities to think things through. It was plain to see that Grandmother Maxwell had many fixed ideas. She thought, for example, that when some mischance had been cleared up, she would come into a lot of wealth.

I knew she wouldn't, but I never argued with her—not because I was afraid of her but because I knew that about most things she couldn't change her opinion even if she had wanted to, which she mostly didn't. And her opinions had nothing to do with why I loved her.[12]

People will differ, come what may. That is a lesson to be learned early.

And children learn it, too—they must to hold to their own way of behaving when it feels right to them. The nine-year-old Slocum boy, in *Something Happened,* just doesn't have the competitive spirit. "Why don't you be what everyone wants you to be? And do what they want you to do?" Fast as he is in the relay, Slocum junior laughs and stops to wait for the laggards to catch up. It is more fun to be together than to beat someone.[13]

Acting Together

When they are free to do so, children often combine forces in a simple version of Rousseau's "social pact," with each of them putting

[10] Stuart Cloete. *A Victorian Son: An Autobiography.* New York: The John Day Company, Inc., 1973. p. 174.

[11] Elizabeth G. Flynn. *The Rebel Girl: An Autobiography.* New York: International Publishers Company, Inc., 1973. p. 46.

[12] William Maxwell, *op. cit.,* p. 199.

[13] Joseph Heller. *Something Happened.* New York: Alfred A. Knopf, Inc., 1974.

"in common his person and his whole power under the supreme direction of the general will." It is from "this act of association" that the group receives "its unity, its common self, its life, and its will."[14] Children have to learn that acting together is the only way to get some things done.

Sometimes after their father had died and been secretly buried up on Old Joshua, it seemed to the proud Luther children that the Lord must have forgotten them. But they kept together, wildcrafting and making Christmas roping, and held out against the hard winter until they found the kind of help they could agree to accept. Then "Trial Valley turned tender green" again.[15]

Next year coed tennis and volleyball classes will be offered at Jefferson Middle School because eleven-year-old Barbara and her friend Sally got petitions going. Who wants to have to choose only between modern dance and something called "slimnastics"? And as Barbara also found out, acting together is what it takes to get state laws changed. She became the first girl paper carrier in Fair Park.[16]

Common action is the route to many kinds of satisfaction that elude the individual actor. In her mythic account of a massive retreat of women to a mountain stronghold, Carol Emshwiller has her narrator speak these words, only partly in self-satire:

> Women! (I say Women! like men say, Men!) Women! You are wild and free, shaking your shaggy manes, eyes like stormy skies, bouncing your breasts, sure-footed, savage, silent on the mountains, your whispered battle cries tentatively spoken in the dark, but about to ring out the sunlight.[17]

Children learn early that when we get together, we are much more than one. All of us, at every age, have to keep reminding ourselves that this is true.

Just Being Together

"The child shall have full opportunity for play and recreation, which should be directed to the same purposes as education [that is, full development]; society and the public authorities shall endeavor to

[14] Jean-Jacques Rousseau. *The Social Contract,* 1762. Book 1, Chapter 6.

[15] Vera and Bill Cleaver. *Where the Lilies Bloom.* Philadelphia: J. B. Lippincott Company, 1969. p. 172.

[16] Betty Miles. *The Real Me.* New York: Albert A. Knopf, Inc., 1974.

[17] Carol Emshwiller. "Maybe Another Long March Across China 80,000 Strong." In: *Joy in Our Cause.* New York: Harper & Row, Publishers, 1974. p. 167.

promote the enjoyment of this right." This is part of Principle 7 of the United Nations Declaration of the Rights of the Child (1959).

When they can, children seek out one another just for fun. Let's play house or hopscotch or jacks, jump rope, put up a pup tent in the backyard, climb a tree, ride our bikes, go swimming, go to the store, watch TV. Skills of associating in informal ways are learned through many occasions of getting together for no reason in particular except just to be together.

Children may also learn social content from such easygoing encounters. Findings from a study of children in six cultures "suggest that, throughout the world, two of the dominant personality traits of children between seven and eleven are self-righteousness and bossiness."[18] Older children are quick to help those who are younger through suggestions of what to do and how to do it as well as through reprimands for inappropriate responses.

And perhaps most important of all, free association provides each child with a place and time for developing "a sense of some unsocialized uniqueness," defined by one psychiatrist in these terms:

... creativity, autonomy, spontaneity, unprogrammed ecstasy—all free from adult intrusion. Included here is the right to play, to engage in non-instrumental behavior, to do "useless" things for the sheer fun of it.[19]

It really is all right to be yourself and have fun. In fact, it is good for you.

Associating is a natural power exercised and strengthened in the pursuit of many purposes. All day long when they can children reach out to others in an effort to find satisfaction and meaning in their common experience. Do we do what we should in school to help children associate in ways that are most fully productive? If we are to face up to the challenge of developing an equal rights curriculum, then answering this question honestly may be a good place to start.

A Framework for Change

Reaching out has to be recognized as one of the strongest of the natural drives. "Social ties and connections," in Dewey's language, are

[18] Beatrice B. Whiting and John W. M. Whiting. *Children of Six Cultures: A Psycho-Cultural Analysis.* Cambridge, Massachusetts: Harvard University Press, 1975. p. 184.

[19] Paul Adams. "The Infant, the Family, and Society." In: Paul Adams and others. *Children's Rights: Toward the Liberation of the Child.* New York: Praeger Publishers, 1971. p. 90. Copyright © 1971 by Paul Adams.

"inevitable" as well as "natural."[20] Surely we hardly need to argue further the case for making better use of associating in providing a new deal for children who have suffered from being undertaught, over-taught, mistaught, or not taught at all. Children will get together whether we want them to or not. They must do so if they are to learn to cope with their world. Our problem is how to guide or direct this getting together so that it works to enliven learning all along the line.

Adventuring, as we have defined it, can broaden the base of school experience for many children. Mastering, if we take it both literally and seriously as a way of learning equally good for and open to all, can release children by the millions from the bondage of no-can-do. What then is the promise of associating?

The essence of this promise is to be found in the nature of common schooling. In his final report to the Massachusetts Board of Education, Horace Mann felt obliged to remind his board of the charge upon state schools. "The very terms *Public School* and *Common School* bear upon their face that they are schools which the children of the entire community may attend." (*Twelfth Annual Report,* 1849). Thus, sectarianism —which was the point at stake—had to be ruled out.

Today the issue of religious sectarianism, while still alive, seems to be fairly well contained. But social sectarianism is something else again. Do we need the federal courts to tell us that the children of "the entire community" are not really getting together in the common schools?

"The soul selects its own society,/ Then shuts the door." This is Emily Dickinson, reflecting on personal "affinity," as it might have been called then (c. 1862).

> I've known her from an ample nation
>   Choose one,
> Then close the valves of her attention
>   Like stone.[21]

How beautiful—if we have intimate friendship or love in mind. But how ominous if we are thinking about associating as the context and content of children's learning. The problem now, as in Mann's day, is to keep the valves of our attention from closing against the children

[20] John Dewey. *Theory of the Moral Life.* New York: Holt, Rinehart and Winston, Inc., 1960; first published 1908, 1932. p. 79.

[21] Emily Dickinson. "The Soul Selects Her Own Society." In: F. O. Matthiessen, editor. *The Oxford Book of American Verse.* New York: Oxford University Press, 1950. p. 416.

of an ample nation—to keep our doors truly open to the children of "the entire community."

Free association among children of the entire community is a legal right determined by the courts. Professionally most of us would agree that association with or among children who differ personally and socially is needed to ensure or enrich many kinds of valued learnings (see Exhibit 12). For our purposes here, we will take the right and value of free and open association for granted—and turn our attention to what it takes to make more of associating with others as context and content in the schooling of children.

Exhibit 12. Differences Among Children as Resources for Learning

Kinds of Differences	Possible Learnings To Be Gained from Other Children
I. *Personal differences*	Range of interests and competencies within each sex
	When all children like to get together
Sex	How others feel about gender roles
	When sex stereotyping gets in the way
	What it would be like to have a brother (or sister)
Age	Kinds of attention young children want
	What is hard for children to learn
	How to help without being bossy
	What it would be like to have an older sibling
	When agemates need each other
Health or well-being	Getting used to being bigger or smaller than others
	Ways to let off steam
	Why some children get tired or fall asleep
	How to make the best of glasses or hearing aid
	What to do when feelings have been hurt
Personality	Why some children try to act funny all the time
	How to get someone to listen
	When to stop teasing
	What to do when someone is too bossy
	Ways to get acquainted with children who do not seem to need friends
Interests and talents	Pets that do not cost much
	Where to find walnuts and wild blackberries
	What makes a good stamp collection
	Getting and using a public library card
	What it takes to become expert at tossing baskets, tumbling, or dancing the polka

Kinds of Differences	Possible Learnings To Be Gained from Other Children
Life experience	Where babies come from
	Changes in living that come from moving to new climate
	When people get married in church
	How to camp out while traveling
	What happens when somebody dies
II. *Social differences* Family setup	Families that are smaller or larger in membership
	When one parent is in charge
	How it is when mother stays home all day
	Brothers and sisters who are younger or older
	What it is like to have grandparents in the home
Racial-ethnic membership	Holidays celebrated by other children
	What another language sounds like
	Heroes who deserve to be more widely known
	How skin color and other aspects of physical appearance can vary among children
	Racial-ethnic sensitivities to be respected
Place of residence	Games that can be played in the street
	What living in a house is like
	When children help with the chores—gathering eggs, hoeing the garden, etc.
	How to go some place on the bus or subway
	Where everybody goes to the same church
Class	How other girls and boys may be expected to behave
	Things to do with leisure time
	How to get the better of somebody mean and hateful
	Terms for body parts and functions; favorite expletives
	What we want to be when we grow up
Income	Where money goes—why we need it
	What unemployment means
	How other children get their spending money
	When somebody holds down two jobs
	When both parents work
Parental occupations	Ways to make a living—office, factory, shop
	How milk gets to market, what the police do, etc.
	When a parent works at night
	When a job transfer comes—how children feel about it
	Women in new kinds of jobs

Associating as Context for Learning

Reaching out to others is natural and necessary. Getting in touch, comparing notes, keeping in touch with others but still maintaining one's own point of view, uniting forces when something needs doing, getting together just to be together—these are behaviors we have cited as illustrations of what children learn as they exercise and strengthen the power of associating. Helping children to associate peacefully and productively has always been a major concern of ours. But perhaps today we are better informed about the importance of combining chil-dren in different ways for different kinds of learning.

Pairs. Younger and older children can be paired for a variety of instructional purposes: to read aloud and listen to what is read, to dictate stories and record them, to tutor and be tutored. At the same time, other learnings possible only from inter-age association may make them-selves evident (see Exhibit 12).

Children closer in age or competence can be paired for many activities, too: joint projects in the subject areas, turnabout practice and test sessions, the playing of instructional games, shared responsibility for housekeeping duties. The possibility and nature of attendant or collateral personal-social learnings will depend upon who is paired with whom—but the range seems limitless.

Small groups. When three children work together as compared to two, the opportunity for learning from as well as with another person obviously increases. In a group of three, the person-to-person relation-ships triple. In a group of four, they number six; in a group of five, there are ten. The prospect of impact and intimacy declines, but the mix is likely to be more varied.

The relationships among several children thus form a context for learning very different from that of the paired relationship. Many study projects can be sited in the small group. But in addition the group itself becomes an arena for learnings related to process—getting everybody's ideas in the mix, planning in terms of varied interests, making decisions, and so on.

Whole group. Films, TV programs, live musical or dramatic presentations, and talks by outside speakers are among the kinds of re-sources or experiences that can be appropriately presented to the whole group. Also, the whole group offers a context for a valued set of process learnings: how to engage in discussion, how to conduct a meeting, how to behave as an audience.

Sometimes the whole group, if it is not too large, acts as a unit. Children sing, dance, play games. Or the group engages in opening exercises, hears news of its members, plans a picnic.

The point we are making is that associating in various combinations provides contexts for different kinds of learning. When we want intimacy, we put children together in pairs. When variety is the criterion, we put three to five children together; then we can also help them learn some of the simpler skills of behaving as a group. For common experiences and development of the more formal group processes, a larger group is needed as context.

Associating as Content of Learning

The natural power of associating is strengthened simply by being exercised. As they have many occasions to get together, children become abler in relating to others and more adept in planning and acting together. In the past, we may have felt that providing such occasions was about all we needed to do. Making it possible for children to associate in school in a variety of contexts must remain where we start. But we can and should do more. If they are to become proficient in associating, children need to learn some things that they may not just pick up along the way. So many of us seem to be saying today.

Understandings. We have identified personal-social differences as resources for learning. These differences can be studied as well as experienced. How do or may sex, family setup, or place of residence bear on behavior? Self-understanding as well as understanding others may be forwarded by looking together at feelings and where they come from and what can be done about getting them out, making use of them, and bringing them under control. Some understandings in the field of social action and politics may be useful to children.

We will return to these and other such understandings when we propose possible extensions of content for an equal rights curriculum. All we wish to do here is to indicate that we know much more about association as a field of study than we may have seen fit to try to teach children.

Skills. We have already noted in our treatment of small groups that children need to learn how to elicit contributions from all members, reach decisions, and so on. Similarly, large groups offer opportunities for other kinds of learning that form a content of sorts. Some of the needed skills may be presented formally, even practiced, to help children use them more effectively. A considerable body of knowledge about group functioning does exist, as we know. Can we do more with it in school?

Attitudes and values. Plainly, we seem to be more aware today than we ever have been that attitudes and values can be attended to directly and effectively. We have always declared ourselves in favor of education in the affective realm. But our ideas about it were vague and inconsequential. Moreover, even if we had known how to get results, we might have hesitated. Indoctrination was a dirty word.

However, we have all learned a great deal over the past ten or twelve years. The focus of our attention on racism, militarism, natural resource abuse, sexism, the oppressive weight of an industrial mass society, and political chicanery and corruption in the highest places has brought attitudes and values of many kinds under scrutiny and debate Does it matter how people look at things? Or what they believe in? You can bet your life—and in some areas of public concern we may have to—that it does.

Teaching for attitude formation and value development in a democratic society would seem to require as context the free association of all children. And if we are to survive and flourish as a people, it would seem to call as well for a content—a set of experiences—that will bring feeling and belief into greater consonance with thought and action.

Intimacy: the Essence of Associating

Children can be put together without really getting very close together. They can encounter content that might make a difference in their relationships without having much chance to do something with it. What we have to do, in short, is to make sure that genuine intimacy gets into the picture and stays there.

Purpose. Is there a good reason for these children to get together? Sometimes in our desire to promote associating, we may settle for a task that could be handled just as well or even better by a child working alone. Children must feel they are getting together because this is the only or best way to do something.

Interaction. How much interaction is really called for? Some tasks can be shared without much intimacy of effort. You do this, I'll do that, and next week we'll get together again. Other tasks call for continuous back-and-forthing between or among children. Phases of a project may differ in this regard. Planning will be more interactive than reporting. No doubt we have to settle for balance here.

Duration. How long will this activity last? An instructional game may be over and done with in 20 minutes. A study project may be carried on for three weeks. Generally speaking, we would expect intimacy to require time for its development. This may suggest that when children are to be paired for quickly completed activities, they should continue as partners for a week or two.

Variety of contacts. How many other children has a given child been able to get close to? Obviously no one child will have an opportunity to work intimately with all the others in a group. But among 25 children the number of possible one-to-one relationships totals 300. For the teacher this means a great wealth of resources to draw on in defining tasks or setting up situations that encourage certain children to come to know one another pretty well.

Such criteria as these can be useful in ensuring that children will get together in ways that forward growth in the power of associating effectively with others (see Exhibit 13).

Children will learn how to associate with others well enough to satisfy their basic needs and make a reasonable amount of sense out of their world. They must develop competence in this highly important

Exhibit 13. Collaboration as a Model of Associating

Element	Exemplification
Purpose	Children are organized in twos and threes to plan and conduct an investigation that will yield information about some aspect of individual differences—strength, reaction time, performance of skills, etc.
Interaction	Each set of investigators selects a topic, plans procedures, collects and interprets data, and prepares a report.
Duration	The children get together regularly over a period of several days to plan and carry through their investigation.
Variety of contacts	Similar investigations have already been engaged in with other partners; more such ventures may be expected to provide chances to work with still other children in the future.

aspect of existence and they do, whether school helps them or not. But with our assistance, they stand a chance of becoming much more effective. Are we willing to try to do more than we have?

Extensions of Content: Some Possibilities

Once again—and for the last time in this manuscript—we face the question that matters most. As far as associating is concerned, what do we think all children need to know? What new content in particular do we propose be added to the curriculum so that more children will be able to come into their own? And why or how do we think it will make a difference?

In answer to these questions, we shall present three areas of new content, the naming of which causes us some uneasiness. As yet, we have not come to a professional agreement on an appropriate language to use. The many creative persons now engaged in exploring these areas are not of one mind about terminology or approach or much of anything else. Also, these are aspects of associating about which in the past our attitude has been hands off. In a way, we have shared the poet D. J. Enright's fear of the prematurely explicit. His child, encountering a peacock on a pathway in Hyde Park, asks its name.

> "The thing that makes a blue umbrella with its tail—
> How do you call it?"

And the poet thinks ahead. Next year, once in school, the "busy discoverer" may be given names in place of adventures in personal definition.

> The dictionary is opening, the gay umbrellas close.
>   Oh our mistaken teachers!
> It is not a proper respect for words that we need
> But a decent regard for things.[22]

Or, in our case, for firsthand associations among children.

Still and all, in these days the spotlight of new knowledge has been turned onto the "unconscious portion of culture," in Trilling's words, and "made it accessible to conscious thought."[23] We now have a sizable

---

[22] D. J. Enright. "Blue Umbrellas." In: *The Typewriter Revolution and Other Poems.* La Salle, Illinois: Open Court Publishing Company, 1971. p. 28. Copyright © 1971 by D. J. Enright.

[23] Lionel Trilling. *The Opposing Self.* New York: Viking, 1955. p. xiv.

body of know-how about the development of personal-social awareness, the development of attitudes and values, and political education— to give tags to our three areas of present concern. We know more, and we are more alert to children's need to know, too. Perhaps we are also more sensitive to the need in our society for greater proficiency in associating. Emerson says it for us: "All are needed by each one;/ Nothing is fair or good alone." ("Each and All," 1835)

Let us examine these new possibilities.

Becoming More Aware of Self and Others

In their exercise of the power of associating, children learn that making demands on other persons works with some but not with all. They find, too, that when grownups want something, compliance usually works better than resistance. In the hurly-burly of everyday existence, the give and take of cooperation becomes the established mode of relating to agemates and elders. Things get done that way. But children also soon begin to seek out relationships that call for a more intimate mode of associating. Persons can get together to create something that does not already exist in their lives and that cannot be developed separate and apart from others. If they will, they can define a goal together, develop plans to reach it, and get going, talking things over as they go. Collaboration of this kind calls for and develops an awareness of self and others that is not possible in the hurried trade-offs that keep things moving in our daily lives. School ought to be one place where such relations can be maximized.

Sharing human experiences. "Whether children's sensitivity should be fostered or discouraged"—that was a theme of interest to Gustave Flaubert and George Sand. They were agreed that children ought to know all of life. "Life must be incessant education; everything must be learned, from talking to dying."[24] The question is academic in the lives of many children. More to our point is the issue of whether children can be helped to learn through sharing their experiences. Sensitivity, consciousness, awareness—whatever it is called, we can say that its extension is at the center of human development. And that sharing through collaborating is the way it is done. "How would it be if one were to choke on oneself?" Kafka wondered. What if "the

---

[24] Gustave Flaubert. *The Selected Letters of Gustave Flaubert.* Francis Steegmuller, translator and editor. New York: Farrar, Straus, & Young, 1953. pp. 218-19.

pressure of introspection were to diminish or close off entirely the opening through which one flows forth into the world"?[25]

Good humor helps. When Mountain Wolf Woman was a child, she went to dig water lily roots in a slough along the Mississippi with the women in her family.

My sister took one of the floating roots, wrapped it about the edge of her blouse, and tucked it into her belt. I thought she did this because it was the usual thing to do. I saw her doing this, and when I happened upon a root I took it and did the same thing. I put it in my belt too. And then everybody laughed at me![26]

Her sister was pregnant, and the root was twined round her middle to ward off something. In this case, teasing was teaching.

And gathering around is a part of it. Before the old man Daylight died, he asked to be taken outside the wigwam to watch the dawn. "Think of me and scatter some tobacco for me. Whatever you want when you do this, it will be granted to you," he told those who had carried him out.[27]

But ridicule can kill. Out of bravado, Richard reports that his father pledges $15 to the Community Chest. The teacher is indignant. "We are collecting this money for you and your kind, Richard Gregory. If your Daddy can give fifteen dollars you have no business being on relief." And not only that: "We know you don't have a Daddy."[28]

What makes us feel good? What hurts us? How can we keep open the channel "through which one flows forth into the world"? The sharing of life experiences in a setting that ensures loving concern and collaboration is where we surely must begin.

Process of socialization. Can children be helped to become more aware of the social forces that may tend to shape some of their behavior? Many persons feel that they can, at least in certain dimensions. Most notable at present is the attention being given to development of gender roles. Consciousness-raising activities here include analysis of stereo-

[25] Franz Kafka. *The Diaries of Franz Kafka, 1914-1923.* Max Brod, editor. New York: Schocken Books, Inc., 1949. p. 223. Copyright © 1949 by Schocken Books, Inc. Reprinted by permission.

[26] Mountain Wolf Woman. *Mountain Wolf Woman: The Autobiography of a Winnebago Indian.* Nancy O. Lurie, editor. Ann Arbor: University of Michigan Press, 1961. pp. 8-9. Copyright © 1961 by the University of Michigan.

[27] *Ibid.,* pp. 17-18.

[28] Dick Gregory with Robert Lipsyte. *Nigger: An Autobiography.* New York: E. P. Dutton & Co., Inc., 1964. p. 45. Copyright © 1964 by Dick Gregory Enterprises, Inc. Reprinted by permission of E. P. Dutton & Co., Inc.

typing in children's literature and TV advertisements, study of the sexist bias in our language and how it is being corrected, examination of the constriction of vocational choices for women, and a review of history for neglected female contributions.[29] It may also include examination of the school program for evidence of differentiated treatment of boys and girls that may limit the "realization of an individual's potentials for expressing, for understanding, for relating, and for experiencing joy." [30]

Career education may be helping to emancipate some children from social restraints on job interests. More than awareness of sex bias is at stake here. School can provide working-class children—and welfare children, too—with models other than those close to home. Ambitions may be aroused. At the same time, a realistic look at occupations may serve to free some middle-class children from the kind of constraints that have kept women from entering the construction and transportation fields even though the pay is better, the working conditions healthier, and advancement more likely than in office or factory; and that may have boxed some boys like Biff Loman into "a phoney dream" of getting ahead by being "well liked" and adventurous, without much reference to either interest or talent.[31]

If the school can become, like the home, one of the primary "systems of open and affective communication," [32] then children will not only learn about new possibilities of behavior but perhaps, in the intimacy of collaboration, begin to spell out for themselves what they think to be the ends of existence to which they may wish to pledge themselves. The goals will change, no doubt. The process of trying to be their own persons continues.

Racial-ethnic differences. A wealth of study materials has been supplied us in recent years for use in helping children of diverse subcultures learn more about the contributions of members of their groups to our common culture. Such materials are useful also, of course, for study by all children. The narrowness of our vision in the past has been limiting all the way around.[33]

[29] See: Barbara G. Harrison. *Unlearning the Lie: Sexism in School.* New York: Liveright Publishing Corporation, 1973.

[30] Richard W. Coan. *The Optimal Personality.* New York: Columbia University Press, 1974. p. 187.

[31] Arthur Miller. *Death of a Salesman.* New York: The Viking Press, Inc., 1949.

[32] Audrey James Schwartz. *The Schools and Socialization.* New York: Harper & Row, Publishers, 1975. p. 157.

[33] See: James A. Banks, editor. *Teaching Ethnic Studies: Concepts and Strategies.* Washington, D.C.: National Council for the Social Studies, 1973.

What are the aims of teaching for awareness in this area? Sometimes we may wonder whether the emphasis in some programs on customs and costumes, language, music and art, food and festivals, and heroes and heroines has not obscured the real problem. At this level, can exchanges between and among children develop and deepen intimacy and collaboration?

Achieving racial-ethnic identity is a worthy goal in itself; no one would deny that. But possibly as a basis of associating with other children, the themes or theses of interaction need to be defined in personal as well as cultural terms. In brief, we doubt that we have done all that needs to be done in this area and thus we include it for creative attention in our new equal rights curriculum.

Like other natural powers, the power of associating is strengthened through exercise. Children are already competent in associating when they come to us, and they will become more so whether we attend to their needs or not. But school can help through provision of selected experiences that will enrich their effectiveness. The content we propose here has to do with becoming more aware of others through associating.

We have contended that children, in a context of intimacy and collaboration, can learn much of importance from sharing human experiences. We propose that children be helped to understand the social forces that may tend to shape behavior in such areas as gender role development and career choice. We urge that continued attention be given to awareness and appreciation of racial-ethnic differences at the personal as well as the cultural level.

New content is coming into existence in the field of awareness education. Shall we see what it can amount to in the better education of children who have been undertaught, overtaught, mistaught, or perhaps not taught some very vital things at all?

Developing Personal-Social Attitudes and Values

Attitudes and values serve to release or restrain interests and energies. An equal rights curriculum must certainly help all children take a close look at what this means. Where do I like to spend my time—and why? Could something else be equally rewarding—or even more so? What is worth working—or fighting—for? This is mine, this is yours: what is ours? What *is* best for all of us? These questions operate in every dimension of association. The creation and clarification of attitudes and values is integral to all schooling whether we are aware of it or not. Today, with the insights of many fields of scholarship to assist us, we seem to be of a mind to attend more directly to this aspect of living together.

Individual valuing. "I am a parcel of vain strivings tied/ By a chance bond together" ("Sic Vita," 1842). Like Thoreau, the child feels, too, that choice is a chancy thing at best. The more venturesome the child, the more the options that come to hand. Satisfaction is of many kinds; answers to puzzlement can come from many sources. The broader the base, the more likely it is that choices will be uniquely rewarding.

Our approach to developing an equal rights curriculum is rooted in broadening this base. Adventuring, as we have defined it, is plainly aimed toward this end. Mastering, we would hope, will be many-faceted. Associating, in our view, needs to be made much of because it is from encounters with all kinds of children that any one child becomes aware of how much there is in the world to enjoy, to puzzle over, to think through. Choosing among goods when there is little to choose from cannot add up to much.

Any classroom can give children a chance to try out some kinds of behavior. Laurie, in Shirley Jackson's story, found the first weeks of kindergarten a good time to test himself against authority. As he reported it to his parents, it was "Charles" who talked out during story hour, hit a boy in the stomach, and was fresh with the teacher. But by the time P-TA meeting came around, Laurie-Charles had come to terms with himself and the situation, with occasional lapses, and was a pretty good teacher's helper.[34]

But as Raths and associates have proposed, children need to choose from, affirm, and act on alternative ways of behaving in many areas of school study and experience if they are to develop values that are personally and enduringly significant.[35] The temptation is always to retreat to a base of behavior that, trouble-related and transient, may invite attention but not repay it. The creation and clarification of values, to be of much importance in the lives of children, cannot be confined to twice-a-week

[34] Shirley Jackson. "Charles." In: *The Lottery.* New York: Farrar, Straus, & Giroux, Inc., 1948.

[35] Louis E. Raths and others. *Values and Teaching.* Columbus, Ohio: Charles E. Merrill Publishing Company, 1966.

talk-it-overs nor entrusted to arise in connection with the learning of conventional subject matter. What is called for is selection of content with value dimensions.[36] In our proposals here, we have tried to include many such possibilities.

Group valuing. The study of moral development in children has attracted renewed attention recently. Piaget's earlier work on the stages by which children may be expected to mature away from egocentrism [37] has been expanded by Lawrence Kohlberg and his colleagues.[38] While not everyone may reach Kohlberg's sixth level, or even his fifth, it has been comforting to learn that natural development tends toward inter-dependence and mutuality.

However, few of us would want to trust entirely to time to take care of value development. In a sense, this would be like counting on the forces of history to bring everything right. A chill in the air tempers our confidence that what ought to be will be. In her glimpse into the future, Doris Lessing imagines a "collapsed" world in which children congregate in dehumanized underground colonies, coming out only to raid upon the remnants of civilized communities.[39] Eugene Ionesco has his nameless hero try to find out what is happening to a world laid waste by war. But telephones do not work, newspapers are no longer published. "I don't understand what's going on and there's no use trying." [40] Modern man may seem to some observers to be retreating "To the dark tideless fields of Nothingness," to use the words of E. A. Robinson ("The Man Against the Sky," 1916).

We must be in agreement, or we would not be thinking together about an equal rights curriculum, that some attitudes and values extend beyond individual choice to become binding upon us all. In this bicentennial year, we ought not to have far to seek to have our common commitments enlivened for us. Benjamin Franklin, realist and patriot, may serve as a sample source:

[36] Sidney B. Simon and others. *Values Clarification.* New York: Hart Publishing Company, Inc., 1972. pp. 20-22.

[37] Jean Piaget. *The Moral Judgment of the Child.* M. Gabain, translator. New York: The Free Press, 1932.

[38] L. Kohlberg and E. Teriel, editors. *Recent Research in Moral Development.* New York: Holt, Rinehart and Winston, Inc., 1973.

[39] Doris Lessing. *The Memoirs of a Survivor.* New York: Alfred A. Knopf, Inc., 1975.

[40] Eugene Ionesco. *A Hell of a Mess.* New York: Grove Press, Inc., 1975. p. 151.

The idea of what is true merit should . . . be often presented to youth, explained and impressed on their minds, as consisting in an inclination joined with an ability to serve mankind, one's country, friends and family; which inclination is (with the blessing of God) to be acquired or greatly increased by true learning; and should indeed be the great aim and end of all learning.

Proposals Relating to the Education of Youth in Pennsylvania (1749)

Children have to create and clarify social commitments for themselves. Associating in intimate and collaborative work and play relationships, they may be expected to come to understand the need for rules, the importance of fair play, and so on.

Perhaps, if we use our full intelligence in the matter, they can also be provided with focused experiences in looking at the larger versions of these everyday guidelines to peaceful and productive living. To what extent can children begin to concern themselves about justice, liberty, integrity, honor, democracy, law, equality, compassion, rights, and responsibilities?

Learning How the System Works

Children do learn much about living and working together in a school that provides for free and open association. They also pick up, from adults and older children and from TV, a considerable amount of information about our political system and how it works, as well as an awareness of conflicting attitudes and values about the law and its enforcement, the courts, the presidency, government control and spending, and the like. Most children, however, get very little direct help in transcending the limitations of their own experience in this area and making more sense of it all.[41] This is one aspect of life about which we would contend that most children have not been taught much of anything. Here equal rights means something more for all children in the way of political education.

Study of activism. "All animals are equal but some animals are more equal than others."[42] After this new commandment had been posted at Animal Farm, the pigs began to walk on two feet, smoke cigars, and talk about "the lower animals." Not every revolution ends

[41] See: Robert D. Hess and Judith V. Torney. *The Development of Political Attitudes in Children.* Chicago: Aldine Publishing Company, 1967; and David Easton and Jack Dennis. *Children in the Political System.* New York: McGraw-Hill Book Company, 1969.

[42] George Orwell. *Animal Farm.* New York: Harcourt Brace Jovanovich, Inc., 1946. p. 123. Permission granted by Mrs. Sonia Brownell Orwell and Secker & Warburg.

this way. But hard-won rights have to be defended to be extended. Slavery is abolished, women win the vote, labor is allowed to organize. What then?

Children can be helped to understand this truth by studying activist movements in our history. Not all the pioneers were woodsmen or settlers in the West. Frontiers have existed everywhere and still exist. Heroes and heroines come from all walks of life, and they are all around us. The eye of conscience is the eye that has learned to see, perhaps with the help of such photographs as those taken by Jacob Riis of the slums and immigrant poor or by Dorothea Lange of the dustbowl migrants.[43]

Advocacy: today's scene. "We are made afraid by a standard of conduct we know to be rare," Robert Coles suggests, in trying to account for our lack of aggressiveness in behalf of our own interests. "What might we do if we were braver?" Children looking at today's scene can learn a good deal about areas in which ordinary persons have tried to get some things done that really take doing—taking on Union Carbide, for example, or strip miners or food wholesalers or manufacturers of children's flammable nightwear.[44]

The impact of Ralph Nader on our understanding of how to organize to set things right has been felt in almost every American community. Children can be helped to become acquainted with the work of public advocacy groups in automobile safety, land use, food processing and packaging, white-collar crime, corporate "welfare," pension systems, and care of the aged, among other widely supported concerns to which Nader and associates have called our attention.[45]

Power resides in many places: the government, business and industry, churches, ethnic groups, professional organizations, educational and cultural institutions. But ultimately power rests with the people. The demand, as Kenneth Clark has so often and so movingly reminded us, is for democratic and rational planning that will bring into some sort of proper balance the will of the people and the know-how of what used to be called vested interests.[46] Children can begin to understand some-

---

[43] Milton Meltzer and Bernard Cole. *The Eye of Conscience: Photographers and Social Change.* Chicago: Follett Publishing Company, 1974.

[44] Colman McCarthy. *Disturbers of the Peace.* Boston: Houghton Mifflin Company, 1973. Foreword by Robert Coles, p. xv.

[45] Hays Gorey. *Nader and the Power of Everyman.* New York: Grosset & Dunlop, Inc., 1975. pp. 45-48.

[46] Kenneth B. Clark. *Pathos of Power.* New York: Harper & Row, Publishers, 1974. p. 83.

thing of what this means by simply being urged to listen to who is talking most of the time on TV and in the press. Who speaks for whom?

Children's rights. Mankind, according to the preamble of the U.N. Declaration of the Rights of the Child, "owes to the child the best that it can give." In recent years, the definition of children's rights under the law has been stepped up. When should the community decide that present provisions for children are inadequate and begin to act? "We are too timid," one expert contends.[47] But undoubtedly we have made gains.

To what extent may it be appropriate for children to be made aware of and become concerned about children's rights? Some persons, who view childhood as a time of exploitation, have proposed that children's rights should be broadened to include responsive design (reachable drinking fountains), alternative home environments (with multiple parenting as one option), and sexual freedom, along with the more familiar rights of freedom from physical abuse and access to schooling.[48] Consulting with children themselves about what they consider to be their rights might provide us with clues as to whether this approach would be rewarding.

Could children profit from study of changes in their lot? Free schooling, child labor legislation, family assistance for dependent children, child care centers, children's clinics and hospitals, state institutions for children, special education programs—these could become topics or themes for such a study.

Action projects. Insights and ideas need the test of action, we are agreed on that. To Peter Blue Cloud, young poet of the Mohawk tribe, a dead hawk nailed to a barn door becomes a symbol of incapacity to which most of us can respond:

> . . . your hollow eyes and tight closed
> talons in last grasping, nailed through wing muscles,
> head down to side, crucified,
>   curved beak slightly open to my own questions
> who has lost another particle of faith.[49]

---

[47] Albert E. Wilkerson, editor. *The Rights of Children: Emergent Concepts in Law and Society.* Philadelphia: Temple University Press, 1973. Summary by the editor, p. 306.

[48] Richard Farson. *Birthrights.* New York: Macmillan Publishing Co., Inc., 1974.

[49] Peter Blue Cloud. "Hawk Nailed to a Barn Door." In: Kenneth Rosen, editor. *Voices of the Rainbow: Contemporary Poetry by American Indians.* New York: The Viking Press, Inc., 1975. pp. 140-41. Copyright © 1975 by Kenneth Rosen.

"If you want knowledge, you must take part in the practice of changing reality," advises Chairman Mao. "If you want to know the theory and methods of revolution, you must take part in revolution." [50] Our own great leader, John Dewey, might settle for evolution but would place the same emphasis on the need for action. Goal-reaching is less important than goal-seeking. "We set up this or that goal to be reached, but *the* end is growth itself." [51]

When we propose that action should culminate the experiences designed for the political education of children, we know that range and intensity will be at issue. Children can be caught up in some aspect of advocacy, perhaps the analysis of Saturday morning advertising or the packaging and pricing of snack foods at nearby stores. What might they do then that would represent further action?

Or study of their rights could inspire children to collect data on sources of income (allowance, chores, gifts, etc.) among classmates or schoolmates. If they came up with a picture of dramatic differences that they felt should be corrected, where would they go to make their complaints known? And should children's lib activities be countenanced in the first place?

Sometimes the school offers itself as an arena for political action. Student council activities may be enlarged to include more than learning about how to campaign for offices, hold an election, or conduct a meeting. Children's demands have ranged from changes in the lunch menu (tortillas instead of bread) to better sharing of facilities (more swimming pool time for the kindergarten). Familiar schoolwide projects have included getting a traffic light, increasing bookmobile service, and working out a tutorial program with students of a nearby high school.

The school neighborhood may become the site of still other activities. Alley cleanups, plant-a-tree days, stay-off-the-lawn campaigns have sometimes brought children and adults together in projects of mutual interest. In some communities, parents and children have combined forces to plan after-school or summer recreation programs. Now and then, when they have had advice from a person as imaginative as Jay Beckwith in the San Francisco area, they have transformed playgrounds

[50] Philippe Devillers. *What Mao Really Said.* Tony White, translator, New York: Schocken Books, Inc., 1969. pp. 123-24. Copyright © 1969 by Macdonald & Co. (Publishers), Ltd. Reprinted by permission of Macdonald & Co., Ltd. and Schocken Books, Inc.
[51] John Dewey. *Theory of the Moral Life, op. cit.,* p. 172.

by replanning them and constructing wooden superstructures—ramps, ladders, platforms, wide slides—to forward creative and cooperative play.[52]

Summary and Conclusion

We need to make much of associating as context and content in our new curriculum.

Reaching out to others is both natural and necessary. Of all the powers children are born with, associating is first on the scene and continues to be foremost in the early years as a means of achieving satisfaction from and making sense out of experience. In the construction of an equal rights curriculum for children, associating offers us a content for learning that promises to make the most of differences among children. When certain kinds of content are at hand, associating should become more enriching and rewarding. Toward this end we have proposed extending content to include more attention to what we know about how personal-social awareness develops, the creation and clarification of attitudes and values, and political education.

We honor associating as a force in children's lives that provides a testing ground for all kinds of life-related learnings.

We propose that different kinds of association be set up to ensure free and open interaction.

We urge that intimacy be ensured by making it possible for children to work together in truly collaborative relationships.

We propose that selected content that deals specifically with more effective associating be added to the curriculum.

Children have much to learn that can only be learned from and with one another in free and open association. We believe this to be true of some and perhaps many of the children who now learn too little of what we try to teach. Goal-setting, time use, habits of work—these may be best learned as children work and study together. Associating provides, too, a corrective base for children who may have been mistaught about gender and other limitations. And, as we have tried to indicate, new content on self-and-others awareness, attitudes and values, and politics will extend the understandings of many, possibly most, children who have not been taught some very vital things at all.

[52] See: Jeremy Joan Hewes. *Build Your Own Playground!* Boston: Houghton Mifflin Company, 1974.

On Our Way

Adventuring, mastering, and associating: these, then, are to be the vital elements of our equal rights curriculum for children.

At present, too many children do not learn what we teach. More than a few learn it too well at the expense of expanded possibilities. Far too many are mistaught, picking up wrong ideas about who they are and what they can do and where their true interests lie. And many, perhaps most, of our children are not taught some things at all that would surely enrich their existence and might change their lives.

Our purpose here has been to propose changes that will make for more successful learning by all concerned. All children, we have contended, have the same right to do well in school. We have gone even further to claim that all children have an equal right to profit fully from a broadly based school program.

In our final chapter, we will sample some of the things schools are already doing to move in the directions we have identified as desirable. Then we will propose extensions in terms of what we think should come next. In conclusion, we will return to the charge and the challenge: Are we ready to do what we can?

Current efforts to make more of adventuring, mastering, and associating are many. The examples that follow are drawn from a dozen or so city, county, and state school superintendents' newsletters. They are offered as representative, of course, rather than as exemplary. Yet they

113

serve to indicate the concern that now exists for strengthening the present program along these lines.

Adventuring on the Current Scene

During a month-long summer environmental science program, 36 Newton, Massachusetts, junior high students took a canoe trip down the Neponset River, explored the upper Charles River, and made a one-day tour of Boston Harbor.

A new challenge at one of the Newton Creative Arts Centers last summer was provided by the moving in of a ton of dirt for a large-scale earth sculpture. Rainfall added to the excitement.

A summer program at Pittsburgh's Frick School adopted the theme, "Pittsburgh Is Some Place Special." Field trips included visits to Fort Ligonier, the Historical Museum of Western Pennsylvania, the Mellon Institute, and the Stephen Foster Memorial; a historic tour of the city was also taken.

During the first semester last year, classes in the Shaker Heights, Ohio, schools took 448 field trips. Places visited included the county jail, the *Cleveland Press* building, the Playhouse Theater, the Shaker Historical Museum, Severance Hall (concerts), the Cleveland Museum of Natural History, and, regularly, the Nature Center.

May study trips by classes at Highland Park School in Grove City, Ohio, included visitation of Blendon Woods, an Amish farm, the public library, and the horticulture department of the high school. Classes were also engaged in activities in the school's own outdoor laboratory.

The "school in the woods" program at Old Hickory Lake, Nashville's outdoor education camp, now provides sixth graders (and fifth graders, when there is room) with chances to dye, card, and spin wool: churn butter; and make candles as well as engage in outdoor activities.

Kindergartners from Wyman School in St. Louis had a chance to meet and talk with Captain Kangaroo when he visited radio station KSLH.

Heritage Village, on the Iowa State Fairgrounds, includes a sod house and replicas of the state's first church, an early fort, and a country school, as well as over an acre of artifacts in Pioneer Hall. Guided tours are available for student and other groups six months of the year.

A number of children at Seattle's Boren School have had an opportunity to learn urban survival skills in a course taught by Sheila Unlauf, district supervisor of nurses. Content of the course included what to do during a power outage, some first-aid techniques, making emergency phone calls, clothing repair, and taking a bus to visit some of the city's free facilities.

As part of their transportation study, 60 second graders from Tacoma's Lyon School made a one-day Amtrak jaunt to Portland, Oregon, and back.

Tacoma sixth graders regularly spend a week at one of three camps, with classes in survival training, soil analysis, plant life, map and compass reading, and biology. Swimming, boating, and fishing—and singing around a campfire—round out the program.

Tom Tipton's recreational living course at Meeker Junior High, Tacoma, offers basics of hunting, fishing, and survival training in fall and spring terms, regular physical education in the winter. Trips include one to the Cowlitz River and three days at Toutle River, where students learn how to smoke and cure salmon.

Hazel Larson, teacher at Meek School in Portland, Oregon, invited local poets to work with her children in a poetry-writing project. The children's poems were shared through the P-TA newsletter.

The nuclear laboratory of Arizona State University, Tempe, offers student tours that feature attention to measurement of neutron activation (as in pennies) and environmental monitoring programs currently in progress.

Fifth graders from Desert Foothills School made an overnight trip to Pioneer Village north of Phoenix as part of their study of life in early times. The village, a bicentennial attraction, offers buildings, artifacts, and activities representative of pioneer days in Arizona.

Children in Chula Vista, California, spend a week of study at a new multicultural center equipped for group instruction and independent study. The first day is made up mostly of orientation classes. The rest of the week children are free to choose from a variety of related activities.

Mastering on the Current Scene

After work on basic skills is completed each day, fourth graders at Lincoln-Eliot School in Newton spend two hours on an integrated science-language arts-media arts program that includes growing plants and keeping a photographic record of their growth, studying weather and preparing TV weather reports.

In Pennsylvania, the State Department of Education's new Educational Quality Assessment program includes the goal of helping "every child acquire to the fullest extent possible . . . mastery of the basic skills in the use of words and numbers."

Mrs. Shirley Shratter's fourth grade at Morningside School, Pittsburgh, planned and presented a series of three puppet shows on George Washington as boy, general, and president. The children made their own puppets and scenery.

Dedication of the new media center in Toledo's Mayfair School was delayed until its bicentennial mural, painted by fifth and sixth graders, could be completed.

Standardized reading and mathematics test scores for Columbus, Ohio, schools are presented each year to the Board of Education and the public. Progress is noted as well as need for further improvement.

Minimal objectives or expectancies in all the subject fields at each grade level have been developed by the Michigan State Department of Education and are serving as guides to local districts in curriculum development and instructional improvement.

In Nashville teachers agree on this: "The time is at hand for a developmental reading program that will leave nothing to chance, either for the learner or the instructor." An all-out effort is being made to reconstruct the reading program toward this end.

A student performance evaluation model that puts the focus on criterion-referenced testing is being tried out by Alabama's State Department of Education.

Last year Missouri's new statewide testing program involved checking out fourth graders in 30 specific areas of proficiency in reading and also in mathematics. Teachers received printouts showing what each child had mastered and where more help was needed. Also, first graders were tested to identify children with potential reading problems.

At the age of three, a child may be enrolled for half-day sessions in the Austin, Texas, school district's preschool class for children with hearing problems. The class provides learning centers in speech and speech-reading, sense training, and auditory training as well as art, language, and library.

Fort Worth's new gymnastics program provides opportunities at the primary level for children to use the low balance beam and such hand apparatus as ropes, balls, wands, and hoops. Middle grade children have the equipment needed to develop tumbling, balance beam, and parallel bar skills.

Children at South Hills School, Fort Worth, are working with a new supplementary mathematics program based on film slides and records that present content and provide directed practice. The program is organized in 50 levels; children move from one level to the next as they satisfy teachers of their mastery.

The 600-pupil John Muir School in Seattle has a racial mixture of 65 percent black, 25 percent white, and 10 percent Asian, Indian, and other. An all-out skills teaching program has yielded dramatic improvement in mathematics and reading test scores. Changes reflect in part "an awareness of people's rights—parents' power," according to one mother who is also a school employee.

Seattle's new program for the gifted calls for locating such children in all segments of the population. Provisions include interest-based minicourses, attention to creative thinking skills, and intensive in-depth instructional experiences.

Fourth and sixth graders at Tacoma's Manitou School have been receiving half-hour swimming lessons once a week at nearby Mt. Tacoma High School. Instructors are high school students with senior lifesaving certificates.

Parents and other native speakers are assisting in Tacoma's bilingual-bicultural education program, which includes attention to the language needs of gypsies as well as of a newly augmented Korean population.

Tumbling and gymnastics programs for children were offered last summer at four different elementary schools in Tacoma.

When six children at Bridlemile School, Portland, Oregon, asked for something new to do in reading, they were assigned to reviewing new books received by the school library. In a month, the children had reviewed 30 books.

At Tully and Tolson Schools in Tucson, Arizona, gifted children have been brought together to enjoy a program built primarily on independent study. Children write a work plan for each day, usually including a certain amount of time for basics but allowing plenty of room for projects all their own.

By state law, California schools will move into teaching the metric system during 1976-1977 when new science and mathematics textbooks are distributed. Recommendations by an interstate study on metric education have called for making measurement more important in teaching the various subject areas and preparing teachers with 10 to 16 hours of in-service education.

Four courses designed to help teachers develop skills in reading instruction were offered on one University of California regional campus last winter. Covering language development, children's literature, reading in content fields, and problems of teaching reading, the courses can become the base for further work toward a master's degree and a reading specialist's certificate.

Painted fingernails are matched with colored typewriter keys in a typing program at Del Mar Heights School, San Diego County, California. All children are expected to be able to type by the time they reach the fourth grade.

Associating on the Current Scene

Each week last summer 40 different sixth graders from Boston, Brookline, and Newton came together at Tanglewood to study music, theater, dance, and other arts, mingling informally with older students also living and studying at the Berkshire Music Center.

A cultural awareness program developed at Baxter School, Pittsburgh, has been based on the belief that a heightened self-image will do much to raise the aspiration level of children.

The social studies program in Mrs. Conrado's class at Highland Park School in Grove City, Ohio, last year included a unit on race and social discrimination and another on conflict. Role-playing as well as discussion helped develop and sharpen main ideas.

Children at Glendale-Feilbach School, Toledo, grew wildflowers from seed and then transplated them in the woods behind their new school, along with pine and spruce seedlings.

In a spring "Trash-a-Thon" sponsored as part of Toledo's environmental education program, students and others cleared 26 neighborhood parks of some six tons of debris.

Classes from the Columbus, Ohio, schools planning to visit such places as the Ohio Historical Center or the Columbus Gallery of Fine

Arts or the Center of Science and Industry are now scheduled so that at any given time the racial mix will represent city-wide enrollment.

Children can become partners in crime prevention. This is the thrust of a St. Louis Police Department's project to acquaint students with such programs as Operation Ident, Crime Blockers, and Citizens' Reserves.

The multicultural Springboard to Learning Program of the St. Louis schools, more than a decade old, offers children opportunities to know persons from other lands and to study their cultures. Last year 11 teachers from foreign countries worked in the program.

Stix School, St. Louis, won the mayor's Beautification Trophy for cleaning up a vacant lot and transforming it into a park by planting trees, grass, and flowers. Children also distributed trash-can lids in the neighborhood.

Courses for teachers in the role of law in our society and individual rights and responsibilities have been developed by the Missouri Bar Advisory Committee on Citizenship. In the courses, teachers develop materials for use with their own students.

A new program in Clinton, Iowa, allows junior high school students to take part in twice-a-week tutoring of children in an elementary school.

A new program in Sioux City, Iowa, schools aims directly at developing self-awareness, cultural and ethnic pride, career awareness, and awareness of moral and ethical problems. A corps of consultants in the program work mainly with individuals and small groups on a great variety of awareness activities.

Contributing 85 bags of collected trash, Meecham Middle School won last year's award in the Litter Pickin' Day sponsored by the Committee for a Greener-Cleaner Fort Worth.

At Concord School in Seattle, Johnny Paddock, an 11-year-old Navajo, is serving as bow-and-arrow consultant in the cultural heritage program. Johnny is state archery champion in his age division.

Children in grades three to five at Portland, Oregon's Irvington School took part in a month-long energy conservation contest. Prizes went to classes in which the most checklists on home use were returned.

Audrey Cornell's first graders at Catalina School, Alhambra District, Glendale, Arizona, study wise marketing as part of their foods unit. They learn to read labels for such information as name of product, weight or volume, ingredients, name of company, and picture of contents.

The children at San Jacinto School, Riverside County, California, develop career awareness by sharing information about what their parents do. Pictures of parents at work are displayed in the classrooms. Parents may come to talk with the children. Sometimes they invite children to visit them where they work.

A new bicultural-bilingual program in San Diego is aimed at developing awareness of Philippine culture, customs, and traditions.

One of the older groups at Sunnyside School in Chula Vista, California, has organized itself as a miniature municipality, with political parties, public officials, taxes, and the like.

In their study of Native Americans, children of one of the Fallbrook district's schools in San Diego County made a totem pole, shell necklaces, reed mats, clay pots, and masks. They also were hosts to a group of 12 children from Santa Ysabel Reservation who presented tribal dances.

How to help children learn interpersonal social skills is the focus of a program that has been in operation several years in six of San Diego County's school districts. Workshops and curriculum manuals assist in developing teaching competence in this area.

After a summer urban studies program, students at two San Diego junior highs made a formal appearance before City Council requesting drainage of a pond located behind an elementary school, erection of traffic signals at a heavily used intersection, and better neighborhood lighting in one area.

Again, these goings-on are drawn from newsletters that happen to have crossed our desk. The activities vary greatly. Several report actions at the state level. Quite a number reflect federal financing of approved programs. Many simply tell of what ahead-of-the-game districts or schools within districts are up to. More than a few honor the creative enterprise of individual teachers. All of these happenings have been considered newsworthy by the editors of the publications in which they were found. We consider them to be so, too. Something is going on out there.

Good as these beginnings are, they are only that. No one claims to have taken more than the first step toward broadening the base for children's learning, revitalizing the drive for mastery, or making the most of collaborative learning. Thus, we seek indulgence for our own attempt to think ahead in each of the areas. If we really want to and are willing to work hard enough, where may we go?

Broadening the Base for Learning

Adventuring provides children with some experiences good in themselves, information and ideas that may be relevant to a variety of subject fields, and certain insights and understandings that bear directly on the quality of a particular environment—nature or our built environment or the cultural realm, to refer to those selected for our earlier attention (Chapter 2). When it offers children genuine interaction with a rich, varied, and spacious environment open to options, adventuring discloses new worlds for all children. Those who do not always learn what we teach are caught up by being where they have not been before and having time to explore what they find there. Those who too often tread water while they wait for something new may find it. Those who have been learning more than is good for them about neatness and niceness can escape into contacts both more vital and more vigorous. Those who have not known as much as they might about the piece of the world in question—and that could include many of our children in relationship to some environments—may get something that will enlarge and enrich their lives beyond all imagining.

As we view it, we need a broader base of life-related learning for our equal rights curriculum. We are already on our way to opening up the school outward, as the activities we have cited would indicate.

Reasons for Adventuring

Why go adventuring anyway? Sometimes the reason is obvious enough. All children enjoy a day at the zoo. And they ought to know where the public library (or its nearest branch) is located. Attendance of a performance at the children's theater will certainly be worthwhile. The second graders' visit to the Plain City Farm always pays off. No one quarrels with the value of sending children to have a look at the art museum, the newspaper plant, or the waterworks.

Probably most of the field trips being taken today are still of this kind. Established as worthwhile in themselves or directly related to study topics (food, communication, etc.), such adventuring tends to become a regular part of the program. But today we are moving into something larger than this.

Study. The week at camp is the most familiar example we now have of study in the field. Driving through the countryside to see the meadows in May or the hills in October is one thing. Settling in for a school-in-the-woods experience is something else again.

The reasons for field study will vary as they should. At present, most of these adventures are related in one way or another to environ-mental education. Children become concerned about water pollution, collecting and analyzing samples from pond and stream. They think together about conservation, undertaking to assay interrelationships in a given biotic community. Or they consider the problem of population control, charting the growth prospects of living things that coexist in the same natural setting.[1]

Use. Another kind of interaction on the increase is that in which use is made of the environment for a purpose that goes beyond simply learning more about it. Here physical education and recreation provide us with the best examples. Sometimes an experience in use is short term —swimming, for example, or sailing, or fishing. At other times, an activity may run through several days. Hiking can call for overnight camping out, woodcraft training may take more than a day or two; survival training, canoeing, riding can become programs in themselves. By definition, outdoor education depends on a natural setting for its existence.[2]

Service. Adventuring and associating come together in certain community service projects.[3] Most familiarly these projects are sited in either the natural environment (cleaning up streams) or in the built environment (collecting trash from alleys and parks). Thinking through the possibilities will no doubt enlarge the range of service projects. No school or district would want to confine adventuring (or associating either) to anti-litter activities, important as these may be.

Our first challenge, then, is to define clearly the good reasons there are for children to venture out into the larger world. As we are finding, interaction with the natural, built, and cultural environments has more than immediate satisfaction to offer. (See Exhibit 14 for sample ideas.)

[1] Larry L. Sale and Ernest W. Lee. *Environmental Education in the Elementary School.* New York: Holt, Rinehart and Winston, Inc., 1972.

[2] See: Charles L. Mand. *Outdoor Education.* New York: Pratt, 1967.

[3] See: Laurence W. Aronstein and Edward G. Olsen. *Action Learning: Student Community Service Projects.* Washington, D.C.: Association for Supervision and Curriculum Development, 1974.

Exhibit 14. Reasons for Adventuring: Some Examples

Reasons for Adventuring	Examples of Activities		
	Natural Environment	Built Environment	Cultural Environment
Study	Testing water Examining soil Mapping terrain Noting evidence of erosion Identifying plants and trees Recording birdcalls Locating and describing animal homes Examining brush fire damage	Mapping area by type of housing Checking on traffic flow Comparing working conditions: office, factory Checking on food prices Observing court procedures Identifying building styles Comparing city's parks and playgrounds	Tracing development of farm tools Visiting Indian mounds Taking on-foot tour of old part of town Attending children's concert Seeing play rehearsal Watching artists or craftsmen at work Talking with author of children's books
Use	Swimming in creek or pond Camping out Collecting fossil samples Collecting tadpoles Gathering nuts Planting garden Making a nursery (seedlings) Catching and smoking fish	Swimming in pool Playing games on public playgrounds Picnicking in neighborhood park Checking out library books Learning to mount butterflies (natural history museum) Visiting seasonal garden display	Borrowing prints (museum) Taking music lessons (arts center) Rehearsing and putting on play (children's theater) Working with poet (on loan from arts center) Taking part in archeological dig (pioneer village site) Learning Mexican dance (multicultural center)
Service	Cleaning up along stream Planting pine seedlings Making nature trail Building erosion control dam Clearing rest area of undergrowth Rebuilding brush pile in pond Helping identify and destroy poison ivy	Clearing litter from vacant lot Turning in jars and bottles for recycling Petitioning for traffic light Reseeding school grounds Cleaning up park or playground Working with younger children (museum classes)	Raising money for museum purchase fund Distributing symphony subscription forms Collecting clothing for wardrobe department (children's theater) Helping prepare TV spot announcements of cultural event Contributing books, prints, records to school library

New Sites for Environmental Education

As schools open outward, the need for facilities for environmental learning activities becomes evident. We have already made good beginnings here, but further attention to this need would seem in order.

Community facilities. Many larger communities provide nature education facilities for school use as part of their parks and recreation program. State parks often do the same although their most recent push has been toward resort-type adult facilities, a trend that may need to be countered by educational forces.

Most cultural institutions also provide some school programs. Quite a few business and industrial outfits offer tours and other services to school groups. The prototype of expanded use of community resources found in Philadelphia's Parkway Project Program [4] could lead to an enlargement in the provision of such study facilities.

Shared school facilities. As adventuring sends more and more children out to learn from the real world, we are going to need all the partners we can find. But our best bet will no doubt remain our own development of facilities to be shared among our schools. At present, the school camp is the prime example.

During the late 60's, in the wake of internal redrawing of boundary lines to redress racial imbalance, many school systems found themselves with buildings that could be converted to specialized uses. Federal funds marked for innovation were sometimes used to equip science resource centers, marine laboratories, dance and drama centers, and the like. The multicultural center reported from Chula Vista, California, seems to be of this type.

Dwindling school enrollment has given us additional free space for redevelopment. The facilities for study of the natural environment may need to be built for that purpose or developed in conjunction with park programs. But for exploration of the built and cultural environments, how reasonable it is to assume that we would find good use for centers such as these:

Port or harbor—experiencing what goes on there: tour, talks with officials, study of displays and printed material

Old town—on-foot study of where the city began, visitation of historic sites, examination of old documents

[4] John Bremer and Michael von Moschzisker. *The School Without Walls.* New York: Holt, Rinehart and Winston, Inc., 1971.

Our community—study of maps, exhibits; short tours; talks with city officials

Racial-ethnic culture—study of exhibits of costumes, art; study of collections of music, literature, books of history; visits to places of worship, shops; conversations with community members

Arts—observation of artists at work, activities in workshops, guided visits to neighboring art museum or galleries

Communications—short tours of newspaper plants, radio and TV studios; study of collection of newspapers, videotapes, recordings.

School districts in outlying areas might share the use of such facilities, offering in exchange access to centers they have developed in other fields.

Adventure Areas Within the School

Are we on the way to redesigning school buildings and grounds to provide more room for adventuring? Outdoor learning laboratories, in which a portion of a large site is allowed to revert to natural growth or is planted to attract wildlife, are being developed by a good many schools in suburban or small-city systems. Here and there play areas are being partially redesigned as adventure playgrounds. Quarters for instructional materials centers are standard now for new schools and presumably may be viewed as broadening the base for cultural exploration.

In recent years, we have been much concerned with open education. Yet surprisingly enough, in redesign of our schools, we have worked almost entirely from the outside walls in. We have converted separate classrooms into shared spaces or built open interior buildings.[5] But we have not brought new space into the picture as we might have had we just looked out the window.

Perhaps our next move in openness will be to bring more space into use by creating indoor-outdoor work areas. Quarters for younger children, threes and fours, have long since been laid out to provide an outdoor area for sand and water play and use of wheeled vehicles. In schools for older children, weather stations and birdfeeders have sometimes been developed in shared courtyards. Animal pens, a garden plot,

---

[5] Alexander Frazier. *Open Schools for Children*. Washington, D.C.: Association for Supervision and Curriculum Development, 1972. Chapter 2, "Openness and Space," pp. 10-25.

a greenhouse, a pond, a roofed-over area for constructive arts, surfaced areas suitable for movement activities, games, and the like—we might provide our children with many venturesome extensions of present facilities if we were to do more to unify indoor and outdoor space for study, work, and play.

We are already on our way toward broadening the base for learning. Defining more closely a range of study, use, and service reasons for adventuring may move us along faster. Being alert to what else we may do about locating community facilities or developing our own off-site educational centers should also be helpful. And we might be well advised, as we think further about it, to extend our interest in openness outward to include new space for on-site adventuring.

Revitalizing the Drive for Competence

Children make the world their own as they pursue purposes that have meaning for them. Taking on the world, they find ways to wrest satisfaction from it. They stick with their pursuit as they must if they are to sort out what is happening to them. Only as they mind their own business—the business of coping with life—does competence come into being. From the exercise of their natural powers, children gain increasing effectiveness in identifying choices and making decisions good for themselves and also for those around them. The powers of expressing and responding, relating, finding out, creating, controlling, valuing— these have been given children to start with (see Exhibit 10). And life as it is lived develops and strengthens these powers. When they come to us, children have a lifetime of learning to draw on. We must stand ready to recognize and delight in their proficiencies.

And we must help all children gain what they need to become even more competent. Schooling can make a difference, we agree—and often does. But in the past, a narrowed and devitalized skills program may have left too many children virtually untouched by our teaching. Others may have learned the same thing all over again every year. A good many have learned what they should not have learned. (Does how something looks on the page really matter more than what it says?) For too many children—perhaps most—we may have neglected the range of competencies that a full life calls for.

"Life is the business I would have him learn." This is Rousseau speaking of his student, Emile. We have contended that mastering the world must be a key element in our equal rights curriculum (Chapter 3). As we have reviewed some of the things going on around us, we have found concern for new levels of mastery—in Newton, Pittsburgh, and points south and west. Let us try here to highlight our own conviction that this renewed emphasis must and will actually add up to something.

Rounded Development as Our Goal

The whole child seems to be newly before us today. Over the past 15 or 20 years, we may be thought to have let our historic commitment to rounded development go by the board. Immersed as we were in trying to understand and do better by cognitive functioning, we may have forgotten the rest of the child. What we found, of course, is that when it comes to behavior, the child insists on putting himself back together again. Detached from the hand or the heart, mind does not function very well.

In a recent study of Eskimo schooling, one set of investigators became aware of the boredom and restlessness of boarding school students. Should their poor showing "be attributed more to general unhappiness or to the curriculum"? [6]

Mastering the world, as we now perceive it, calls for a triple-threat approach. Competence is based on control of mind, body, and feeling. And when we neglect any of these, or overlook their interrelationships, we find ourselves in trouble.

Mind. The fundamentals—reading, language arts, mathematics, and science, as we have defined them—are generally thought of as intellect-oriented. Yet the whole burden and greatest strength of our present push is toward building a performance base for the development of skills in these areas. Framed in behavioral terms, objectives are used for both teaching and testing. These are the things children should and will be able to do if we teach well and guard against letting neatness and niceness get in our way. In the southern Indiana of the early 1900's, as Jessamyn West reminds us, "A nice-talking child no doubt felt superior to one who talked of his butt and his belly, who puked instead of vomited, and possibly who even et instead of ate." [7] Power must be prized above propriety.

[6] Carol F. Feldman and associates. *The Development of Adaptive Intelligence.* San Francisco: Jossey-Bass, Inc., Publishers, 1974. p. 107.

[7] Jessamyn West. *Hide and Seek: A Continuing Journey.* New York: Harcourt Brace Jovanovich, Inc., 1973. p. 143.

However, nothing promises to do more to revitalize skills teaching than moving it onto an activity base. Skills develop from purposeful reading, from writing compositions that mean something to the writer, from the practical use of measurement, from inquiry into contrasting diets for white rats or something else that seems important to the investigators. Skills may still be introduced in practice sessions. But developing real competence is seen to depend on setting up situations that require their use (see Exhibit 15).

Body. We are proposing that the constructive arts be included

Exhibit 15. Relationship between Practice and Use of Skills

Skills Areas	Practice of Skills	Application of Skills
The fundamentals	Completing learning packet on metric measurement	Expressing dimensions of display design areas in metric terms
	Doing practice sheet on quotation marks	Writing story containing conversation
	Viewing filmstrip lesson on use of card catalog	Finding materials on transportation study topics in IMC
Constructive arts	Sawing piece of wood after demonstration	Building tugboat for harbor unit
	Measuring out ingredients for small-group cooking project under adult guidance	Preparing batter for drop cookies on their own: parents' tea
	Cutting and joining chicken wire to form square or sphere	Preparing dinosaur framework for science project
Body management	Bending over to make a single somersault	Performing a series of somersaults: gymnastics
	Tossing a ball from one child to another in a circle of widening dimensions	Playing a variety of ball games
	Exploring space in six directions: front, back; side to side; up, down	Incorporating movements in expressive dance
Self-management	Inventing and rehearsing behavior thought to be characteristic of differing dispositions	Role-playing situations derived from reading, study, and real life
	Practicing behavior needed for effective group functioning: supportive, assertive, conciliatory, etc.	Assuming changing roles in group activity, with analysis of variety and flexibility

among the areas in which skills mastery is to be expected. The practical and home arts, arts and crafts, and project work all involve learning to do as well as learning by doing. The physical base of the constructive arts is apparent enough. Their union with the academic areas is part of what we seek as enriching to both.

But celebration of the physical side of children's development is surely a good in itself. The deft hand, the practiced eye, the well-balanced bearing: all serve the child well. Thus it is that we welcome the evidence we have found of field interest in an expansion of the physical education program. Perhaps the frontiers here have to do with movement education and individual sports, particularly gymnastics. But we would urge renewed attention to the possibility of expanding the role of modified team games and sports, too.

Valuing and working hard to develop skills in all these directions is essential if we are to accept well-roundedness as our goal. Moreover, taking the constructive arts and physical education seriously could bring to life many children who may have thought of school as a place designed chiefly for drowsing the midday hours away. Contrived reinforcers of children's behavior, operant conditioners complain, "generally share the troublesome property of evanescence."[8] Can we help them discover that some activities are inherently rewarding?

Feeling. Roundedness would seem to demand that equal time be given the affective realm, to use the jargon of the early 60's. Toward that end, we have proposed adding self-mastery to the range of school-sponsored competencies. As awareness of self develops, a need to work on the skills of self-management may come about. Experience in being an outsider, psychiatrist Robert Coles contends, forwards such self-consciousness among black or Chicano or Indian children and among white Appalachian children who find themselves in Dayton, Cincinnati, or Chicago. An eight-year-old outsider, impelled by "the things he likes to do and wants to do and every single day does do," copes with and comes into surprising control of self and circumstances, everything considered.[9] A childhood in and out of 37 schools in a dozen states gave the elder son of one migrant family ample opportunity to learn about

---

[8] G. S. Reynolds. *A Primer of Operant Conditioning.* Glenview, Illinois: Scott, Foresman, and Company, 1975; revised edition. p. 140.

[9] Robert Coles. *The Mind's Fate.* New York: Little, Brown and Company, 1975. p. 31.

outsiders. By the time of his first social protest arrest at age 14, Cesar Chavez had come to know who he was and what he had to do.[10]

No-nonsense Achievement Standards

Commitment to rounded development is sometimes suspect. Does this mean that we will seek to balance, one against another, differing levels of performance in the areas of valued competence? A child may be a fast runner but a poor reader. Is this going to be all right with us?

Evaluation. If we are to develop an equal rights curriculum that means anything, we will have to come out for strength across the board. Along with group instruction and the attribution of children's failure to learn to nonschool reasons, the normative model of evaluation has lost its hold on us. Our interest in the 20 million pages of test results produced by the National Assessment of Educational Progress is chiefly historical.

Criterion-referenced testing promises to keep no-nonsense standards of achievement before us for all children. The challenge is to try for mastery the first time around. We can flub it by retreating to eventual mastery as our aim. Certain behaviors, we may decide, need to be developed by all children in due time, but all-at-once mastery is too much to ask for.

Debate on this prospect deserves to be intense during the next decade or two. We may find that resolution to succeed with everybody has to precede learning how to do it. That is our own expectation. And it is in this direction that we advocate moving as we work to develop a new curriculum for children. Paying persons inside or outside the profession to get better results, attractive as this has appeared to some of us,[11] may be less productive than a common determination to do what most needs to be done.

Environment. Skill development takes place best in an environment in which children are able to form and pursue meaningful purposes. As we have indicated, introduction and practice of new skills have to be followed by many occasions for application. Obvious as this may seem to be, it is slighted in some approaches to mastery learning. Testing can take precedence over teaching, with the teacher spending

---

[10] Jean Maddern Pitrone. *Chavez: Man of the Migrants.* Staten Island, New York: Alba House, 1971. p. 18.

[11] Educational Testing Service. *Performance Contracting as a Strategy in Education.* Washington, D.C.: Government Printing Office, 1975.

more time giving tests and recording scores than in arranging the experiences requisite for the development of high-level competence.

Advocates of a tightly controlled environment in the teaching of skills have too often misread their own literature. At Walden Two, "subjects" were not taught at all. "We teach only the techniques of learning and thinking."[12] Children, with the run of libraries and laboratories, learned from the pursuit of their own purposes. We must agree that the greatest need of children is a rich environment responsive to their will to learn. As Dewey pointed out so often, freedom "to frame purposes and to execute and carry into effect purposes so formed" is what counts for most.[13] Intelligence in action—that is how children master their world.

What we are advocating is the release of children to range through an expanded environment toward realization of goals that matter to them. Control comes from absorption in the task at hand. Personal involvement governs and shapes behavior better than external efforts at domination. From the hearings before the Senate Subcommittee on Constitutional Rights, we may expect legislation to regulate control practices that have originated in the behavioral sciences. But we do not need to await such action to decide that the best environment to gain our ends is the environment that best enables children to gain theirs. In problem-posing education, as Freire reminds us, teacher and students "become jointly responsible for a process in which all grow."[14]

Making the Most of Collaborative Learning

Children get together to compare notes on what is happening to them and around them. They learn from one another how to hold their own, how to act together. And, of course, they find that just being together is a good in itself. Associating, as we have defined it, is a power that children are born with. But children have much to learn about how to do it well. They learn from working together. They can also learn through the study of selected aspects of human association. In

[12] B. F. Skinner. *Walden Two*. New York: Macmillan Publishing Co., Inc., 1948. p. 98.

[13] John Dewey. *Experience and Education*. New York: Macmillan Publishing Co., Inc., 1938. p. 67. Copyright © Kappa Delta Pi. Reprinted by permission.

[14] Paulo Freire. *Pedagogy of the Oppressed*. Myra B. Ramos, translator. New York: Herder & Herder, Inc., 1970. p. 67. Copyright © 1970 by Paulo Freire. Reprinted by permission of The Seabury Press, Inc.

our new curriculum, we have proposed intimacy as one of our goals, with collaboration as the mode. We assume activism to be another, with socially relevant content as the means.

We hope these commitments have already come through in our treatment of associating as a key element in the new curriculum (Chapter 4). But the examples from the field inspire us to say more. Are we perhaps placing an undue reliance on multiculturalism and cleanup campaigns to create a new level of social sensitivity among children? We think we need to look further at content possibilities. Are we attending enough to the environment for schooling as itself a force in social education? Let us begin our own review with the importance of environment.

Environment as Social Education

We are assuming that the children in a school committed to an equal rights curriculum will be a cross section of the larger population. Even then, unless an appreciation of the educative possibilities of association exists in the school, being together may not mean getting together. Children may sit side by side in the same classroom or teaching area without much contact.

Openness. Space that lends itself to workshop, laboratory, or studio activities; larger blocks of time for work and study; and some degree of independence in deciding what to do and when to do it—these are among the factors that promote getting together. When we add adventures in nonschool environments such as those we have proposed, then we can be sure that children will find many occasions and opportunities for informal person-to-person interaction.

Our point is that we need to be concerned about how much openness is provided by the environment for schooling. By its design, we can help or hinder social education. Frank Lloyd Wright's demand that "American architects must become emancipators of senselessly conforming human beings imposed upon by mediocrity" [15] might be taken to heart by all of us. The architects of his early years, Wright charged, "did not love architecture enough to have it on their consciences." [16] Are we as concerned as we should be about the impact on children of the surroundings we provide for learning?

[15] Frank Lloyd Wright. *A Testament.* New York: Horizon Press, 1957. p. 24.
[16] *Ibid.*, p. 83.

Collaboration. We have proposed collaboration as the model for establishing intimacy (see Exhibit 13). Perhaps it may seem hardly necessary to reiterate our belief in the function of intimacy in learning from as well as with other children. But we do want more than the informal exchanges encouraged by an open environment, valuable as these are.

Children need to have many chances to explore the world on their own terms. We agree on that. But sometimes they need to work and study together—in pairs, in small groups, in the larger group. Intimacy takes time to develop. And some circumstances support its development better than others. Relationships deepen as children get together in pursuit of common ends that can be reached only through acting as well as being together. How vital this is, and how simple it seems.

Proposals for social education that ignore how children are organized for living and learning together in school overlook the richest of possible resources. Can we make sure that our new curriculum is built on a collaborative base?

Value-centered Content

Content counts, too, of course. We have made progress in locating and incorporating content that honors minority racial-ethnic heritages. But are we continuing our search for other new content that may relate to social education? And are we making the most of all the opportunities we may have to center our teaching on the creation and clarification of social values?

Socialization. As a case in point, we may consider the process of socialization. Here is a possible new content area that we have already discussed at some length (Chapter 4). Self-and-other understandings, according to the prevailing theory, are picked up from life around us. We become what we are by assuming roles defined for us—roles that arise from and pertain to such factors as age, gender, and class. Could study of how this happens be helpful to children? "I look at myself as preeminently an emancipator, and I am in sympathy with every emancipation." Can we agree with the great contemporary philosopher of self-determination? "All things in human life should be born of freedom and pass through freedom and be rejected whenever they betray freedom." [17]

[17] Nicolas Berdyaev. *Dream and Reality: An Essay in Autobiography.* New York: P. F. Collier, Inc., 1962. pp. 56, 58.

We have proposed that we can and should concern ourselves with teaching children more about the nature of socialization. Our fear is that interest in the area will be limited to too few dimensions. Awareness training and consciousness raising have led the way. But they represent a larger content that can provide needed perspectives all along the way.

Focus on social valuing. As it must be with adults in any society, concern for the creation and clarification of social values has always been a major factor in working with children. But almost without being aware, we seem to have moved in very recent years toward a more direct commitment in this area. No doubt our directness reflects widely shared anxieties about many aspects of our society. We seem to be more willing to declare ourselves. Who is to stand for the good society if we won't?

At any rate, we have defined many new value-centered content areas as deserving of exploration by children. Ten of these, presented briefly in Chapter 1, we have relied on heavily in making our content proposals for an equal rights curriculum. If we look at the ten areas in terms of opportunities to teach social valuing, we find all of them prime for this purpose (see Exhibit 16).

Exhibit 16. Social Valuing in New Curriculum Areas

Content Areas	Sample Topics of Study
The environment	Control of waste and pollution
	Protection of wildlife
	Preservation of wilderness areas
	Population control
	Design of environment good for all living things
Full range of the arts	The arts and ethnic expression
	Celebration through the arts: festivals and the like
	Public support of the arts
	City planning
	Scope of the arts: our common heritage
Love and friendship	What friendship means
	Conflict resolution: talking it over, working it out
	Patterns of family living
	Skills of working together
	Building bonds with others

Content Areas	Sample Topics of Study
Media and the marketplace	Truth in advertising Children's television programming Children's buying habits Sources and distribution of the news Role of public television
Play and playfulness	Children and team sports Sexism in sports Adventure playgrounds Outdoor recreation areas After-school, weekend, and summer recreation programs
Political action	How laws are made and enforced Nature of public discussion and debate Social movements past and present Political parties Getting something done
Self-understanding	Growth and development of children Process of socialization Development of self-concept Individual differences Talent development
Value clarification	Lives of great men and women Stories in which value conflicts occur Choice of service projects Nature of decision making Great virtues and values: justice, freedom, generosity, etc.
The world of work	Interdependence Worthiness of all work Contributions of various occupations Welfare of workers Child labor: its history
A world view	Nationhood and United Nations World cultures: their variety and richness The developing nations World problems The ideal of world peace

Activism. "We could change the whole of society tomorrow if everybody could agree," a distinguished sociologist observes. However, everyone "is bound into a system of established relationships which to a large extent hamper his will."[18]

We have proposed that children be helped to understand how the political system works. The story of our 200 years as a nation needs to be recast to give more credit to the contributions of minorities and women—and also to recount their struggle for equal rights. Similar attention needs to go to the troubled rise of organized labor, the long debate on the value of public schooling, the plight of the Indians, the drama of the drive for public care of "unfortunates," the continuing clash between private interests and the public interest to be found in the conservation movement. We may wish to provide an even larger perspective for children by alerting them to our role in the world struggle against hunger, disease, ignorance, and repression.

Things do not necessarily have to be as they are. Good things can be helped to happen. Acting in association can make a difference. Even in the most difficult of situations, as Camus contended, "strength of heart, intelligence, and courage are enough to stop fate and sometimes reverse it." As teachers of all the children of all the people, we need "to favor freedom against the fatalities that close in upon it"[19]—and educate children as well as ever we can to do the same.

A Final Word

Children come on the scene blessed by nature with all the powers they need to make the world their own. Adventuring abroad, they find satisfaction in being alive and coming to grips with their experience.

> There was a child went forth every day
> And the first object he look'd upon, that object he became.[20]

From whatever they encounter, children draw what they have to have to sustain and strengthen their natural powers.

Then they come to school.

---

[18] Karl Mannheim. *Ideology and Utopia: An Introduction to the Sociology of Knowledge.* New York: Harcourt Brace Jovanovich, 1936. pp. 260-61.

[19] Albert Camus. *Resistance, Rebellion, and Death.* Justin O'Brien, translator. New York: Alfred A. Knopf, Inc., 1966. p. 141.

[20] Walt Whitman. "There Was a Child Went Forth." In: F. O. Matthiessen, *op. cit.,* p. 276.

When they reach us, children bring with them a lifetime of learning. And we try to provide what will help them become even more competent. For many children, school offers a good deal that they can use. But for some, school does not add up to much. What society is concerned about today is how the school can do better by such children and, indeed, by all children. We are concerned, too.

All children have a right to learn. More than that, we would contend, all children have a right to learn what is most worth learning. Thus, we have been led to define the elements of a curriculum that would be good for all children—an equal rights curriculum.

Adventuring is one of these elements. For too many children, school is a paper-and-pencil prison. Outside, the sun illuminates a world alive with incident and interest. More extensive and intense interaction with the natural and built environments and the cultural realm will broaden the base for learning for children and enliven the whole process.

Mastering is another element. Children must be taught what they need to know and no nonsense about it. Too many children—in particular, those from racial-ethnic minorities, inner-city and up-the-hollow children, the children of the poor, working-class children, children labeled as "dumb," boys as a group—have had a hard time mastering the fundamentals. These are the children we have undertaught. Can our failure come partly from the fact that we have expected such children not to do too well? Could it have been that in times past we really may not have cared enough? Today we *do* expect these children to learn. And we care; we care deeply. We are resolved to find ways to succeed in helping the undertaught to master the fundamentals and much more as well.

Associating is the final binding element. Our concern here is for an extension of the curriculum for all children. Undertaught—and undervalued—children need to learn from and with other children, both in the dimension of work and study behavior and in self-and-other understandings. Children who may have been mistaught about racial-ethnic, gender, and class differences need the correction that comes from interacting with all kinds of children and also from studying the social aspects of human behavior. Most of our children will profit from more attention to such learning.

The equal rights curriculum we propose is meant to be good for children who have been undertaught. It will provide a more vital base for learning, ensure mastery, enlarge the arena of self-and-other learning. It should also be good for children who may have been overtaught. A more open environment with more options and more independence should free overlearners and sitstillers from waiting for teacher direction. The new curriculum should do much to counteract the misteaching of children who may have picked up behavior stereotypes from school or had them go unchallenged and uncorrected there. And hopefully a more venturesome, competency-oriented, value-centered curriculum will bring to all children, from the great wealth of possibilities that surround us, more of what is most worth learning.

All children are created equal. They have the same right to successful teaching. They have the same right of access to the fullness of the human heritage. "What the best and and wisest parent wants for his own child," John Dewey pronounced, "that must the community want for all its children." [21] As we enter our third century as a great nation, let us act to make this dream come true.

[21] John Dewey. *The School and Society*. Chicago: University of Chicago Press, 1899. p. 1.

Author

ALEXANDER FRAZIER is professor of education and a member of the Faculty of Early and Middle Childhood Education at The Ohio State University. He has worked as supervisor and curriculum director in public schools in California, Arizona, and Texas. In 1969-70 he served as president of ASCD. More than 200 of his articles have appeared in educational magazines, and he has edited books for the National Council of Teachers of English and for the Association for Supervision and Curriculum Development. ASCD published his *Open Schools for Children* in 1972, and in 1976 his most recent book, *Teaching Children Today,* was published by Harper & Row.

ASCD Publications, Summer 1976

Yearbooks

Balance in the Curriculum (610-17274)	$5.00
Education for an Open Society (610-74012)	$8.00
Education for Peace: Focus on Mankind (610-17946)	$7.50
Evaluation as Feedback and Guide (610-17700)	$6.50
Freedom, Bureaucracy, & Schooling (610-17508)	$6.50
Leadership for Improving Instruction (610-17454)	$4.00
Learning and Mental Health in the School (610-17674)	$5.00
Life Skills in School and Society (610-17786)	$5.50
A New Look at Progressive Education (610-17812)	$8.00
Perspectives on Curriculum Development 1776-1976 (610-76078)	$9.50
Schools in Search of Meaning (610-75044)	$8.50
Perceiving, Behaving, Becoming: A New Focus for Education (610-17278)	$5.00
To Nurture Humaneness: Commitment for the '70's (610-17810)	$6.00

Books and Booklets

Action Learning: Student Community Service Projects (611-74018)	$2.50
Adventuring, Mastering, Associating: New Strategies for Teaching Children (611-76080)	$5.00
Beyond Jencks: The Myth of Equal Schooling (611-17928)	$2.00
The Changing Curriculum: Mathematics (611-17724)	$2.00
Criteria for Theories of Instruction (611-17756)	$2.00
Curricular Concerns in a Revolutionary Era (611-17852)	$6.00
Curriculum Change: Direction and Process (611-17698)	$2.00
Curriculum Materials 1974 (611-74014)	$2.00
Differentiated Staffing (611-17924)	$3.50
Discipline for Today's Children and Youth (611-17314)	$1.50
Early Childhood Education Today (611-17766)	$2.00
Educational Accountability: Beyond Behavioral Objectives (611-17856)	$2.50
Elementary School Mathematics: A Guide to Current Research (611-75056)	$5.00
Elementary School Science: A Guide to Current Research (611-17726)	$2.25
Eliminating Ethnic Bias in Instructional Materials: Comment and Bibliography (611-74020)	$3.25
Emerging Moral Dimensions in Society: Implications for Schooling (611-75052)	$3.75
Ethnic Modification of Curriculum (611-17832)	$1.00
The Humanities and the Curriculum (611-17708)	$2.00
Humanizing the Secondary School (611-17780)	$2.75
Impact of Decentralization on Curriculum: Selected Viewpoints (611-75050)	$3.75
Improving Educational Assessment & An Inventory of Measures of Affective Behavior (611-17804)	$4.50
International Dimension of Education (611-17816)	$2.25
Interpreting Language Arts Research for the Teacher (611-17846)	$4.00
Learning More About Learning (611-17310)	$2.00
Linguistics and the Classroom Teacher (611-17720)	$2.75
A Man for Tomorrow's World (611-17838)	$2.25
Middle School in the Making (611-74024)	$5.00
The Middle School We Need (611-75060)	$2.50
Needs Assessment: A Focus for Curriculum Development (611-75048)	$4.00
Observational Methods in the Classroom (611-17948)	$3.50
Open Education: Critique and Assessment (611-75054)	$4.75
Open Schools for Children (611-17916)	$3.75
Personalized Supervision (611-17680)	$1.75
Professional Supervision for Professional Teachers (611-75046)	$4.50
Removing Barriers to Humaneness in the High School (611-17848)	$2.50
Reschooling Society: A Conceptual Model (611-17950)	$2.00
The School of the Future—NOW (611-17920)	$3.75
Schools Become Accountable: A PACT Approach (611-74016)	$3.50
Social Studies for the Evolving Individual (611-17952)	$3.00
Strategy for Curriculum Change (611-17666)	$2.00
Supervision: Emerging Profession (611-17796)	$5.00
Supervision in a New Key (611-17926)	$2.50
Supervision: Perspectives and Propositions (611-17732)	$2.00
The Unstudied Curriculum: Its Impact on Children (611-17820)	$2.75
What Are the Sources of the Curriculum? (611-17522)	$1.50
Vitalizing the High School (611-74026)	$3.50
Developmental Characteristics of Children and Youth (wall chart) (611-75058)	$2.00

Discounts on quantity orders of same title to single address: 10-49 copies, 10%; 50 or more copies, 15%. Make checks or money orders payable to ASCD. Orders totaling $10.00 or less must be prepaid. Orders from institutions and businesses must be on official purchase order form. Shipping and handling charges will be added to billed purchase orders. **Please be sure to list the stock number of each publication, shown in parentheses.**

Subscription to **Educational Leadership**—$10.00 a year. ASCD Membership dues: Regular (subscription and yearbook)—$25.00 a year; Comprehensive (includes subscription and yearbook plus other books and booklets distributed during period of membership)—$35.00 a year.

Order from: **Association for Supervision and Curriculum Development
Suite 1100, 1701 K Street, N.W., Washington, D.C. 20006**